MEDIA BIAS IN THE TRUMP PRESIDENCY AND THE EXTINCTION OF CONSERVATIVE MILLENNIALS

How The Mainstream Media Has Stolen A Generation Of Voters

David Keltz

Keltz Publications

*This book is dedicated to my parents, my stepfather,
my grandparents, my brother, and all those who were
indoctrinated by the left, but can now see the light.*

CONTENTS

FOREWORD

Since this book was written, the full contents of the Mueller Report have been released. For two and a half years, the media peddled a fictitious narrative that said unequivocally that President Trump, and the Trump campaign had "colluded" with the Kremlin, in an attempt to meddle in our election. Day after day, CNN, MSNBC, The New York Times, and the Washington Post peddled one "bombshell" story after another that they said would lead to Trump's impeachment.

For months, CNN allowed Democrat House Intelligence Chairman Adam Schiff to come on their program and repeatedly issue false statements, as he did in the fall of December 2017 when he said that: "The Russians offered help, the campaign accepted help. The Russians gave help and the President made full use of that help." Not only was that a blatant lie, but Schiff knew it was false. Just two months earlier in July 2017, James Clapper, the former Director of National Security, told Schiff under oath: "I never saw any direct empirical evidence that the Trump campaign or someone in it was plotting/conspiring with the Russians to meddle with the election." The same was true of other former Obama officials including Susan Rice, Ben Rhodes, and Samantha Power, who all said in private and under oath that they did not find any evidence that the Trump campaign colluded with the Russians. Yet, it did not prevent them from saying the exact opposite on tv, in front millions of viewers to anti-Trump media mob, that was complicit in destroying Trump.

After employing 19 lawyers, 40 FBI agents, more than 2,800

subpoenas, nearly 500 search warrants, interviewing, approximately 500 witnesses, and spending 32 million dollars of taxpayers money, the Mueller Report did not find any evidence that Trump or anyone on his team colluded with the Russians. As the Mueller report stated: "[T]he investigation did not establish that members of the Trump Campaign conspired or coordinated with the Russian government in its election interference activities." The media could barely hide their disappointment at the outcome of the Mueller Report, but they made it very clear that it did not in any way exonerate Trump. As if the role of a special prosecutor was to say that the defendant was "not, not guilty."

Unsure of what malfeasance to accuse Trump of next, the media found a way to blame "his divisive rhetoric," on a mass shooting in Dayton, Ohio during the summer of 2019. Never mind the fact that the shooter identified himself on social media as a leftist, and as an Elizabeth Warren supporter. That was all a warmup act for the next charade. The Democrats and the media created a new charge against the president that was so laughable, even Hollywood would have thrown the script away. Realizing that a special counsel would not save them, the Democrats, led by (you guessed it) Adam Schiff moved to impeach the president.

They contended that Trump had pressured the President of Ukraine, Volodymyr Zelensky during a phone call, to dig up dirt on his likely opponent in the general election, Joe biden. They accused Trump of engaging in a quid pro quo, in which he had withheld aid to Ukraine, in exchange for asking Zelensky to start what they called a phony investigation into Biden's son Hunter, who had served on the board of a Ukrainian natural gas company, called Burisma, where he was paid over $83,000 per month, despite having no experience having ever worked for a gas company. Not only did Ukraine receive the $391 million dollars in aid that had been withheld, but they were not even aware that it had been withheld until one month after the phone call, which undercut their entire argument.

As of this writing, the country has been dealing with a global health pandemic that has now killed 113,209 people in the country and led to 40 million people filing for unemployment in just over three months. After the horrific police killing in Minneapolis of a black man, by a white cop, the media has now found a way to simultaneously blame the president for his handling of COVID-19, (even as the U.S. leads the world in testing, and distribution of personal protective equipment) while also holding him responsible for "systemic racism." So as protestors, rioters, and looters, gather across the country in defiance of social distancing guidelines (that the media seemed so concerned about, just days ago), to destroy businesses, and private property, to set fire to the nursey in the historic St John's Church, just outside the White House, or to spray graffiti on the Lincoln Memorial, and deface confederate statues across the country, the media is willing to overlook lawlessness, and violence, because they see the cause as justified, and they hope that the divisiveness will lead to a Trump defeat in November.

It is for these reasons that Trump has rereferred to the media as the enemy of the people. Similarly, to the Democratic party, they are willing to openly support the downfall of country if it means removing Trump from the White House. If rooting for violence, destruction of property, and high unemployment does not make you the enemy of the people, then I don't know what does.

David Keltz

6/11/2020

INTRODUCTION

Core values and ideologies of Conservatism have suffered irreputable damage as a result of explicit and intentional bias that is prevalent in mainstream media outlets, including the New York Times, Washington Post, CBS, NBC, ABC and CNN. The political agenda of the mainstream media has had an adverse effect on the Conservative party, especially with younger cohorts. Millennials, particularly those with college degrees, are far more likely to identify as left wing or liberal and are more likely to vote for Democrats than to identify as Conservative and vote for Republican candidates. According to the Pew Research Center fifty seven percent of Millennials hold consistently liberal values, while just twelve percent hold consistently Conservative values.[iii] This is especially problematic for the Conservative party, since numerous studies indicate Millennials will surpass Baby Boomers in 2019 as the largest class of voters.[iv] This book will explore clear instances of implicit bias against Conservative principles, figures, ideologies, policies, and agendas across mainstream media outlets, and how Conservatives can combat the national media onslaught that has become so pervasive and prevalent in American society that the views of a small minority of coastal elites have become normalized. It will also analyze the political attitudes of Millennials and outline strategies, tactics, and messaging that Conservatives can use to appeal to this cohort in the 2020 election.

Abstract:

The latest IBD/TIPP poll shows that half of the country says that its trust in the mainstream media has decreased in the last two years and more than two-thirds of Americans believe the media is more concerned with pushing its own agenda than on reporting the facts.[i] According to the Washington Post, only seven percent of journalists identify as Conservative or as Republicans.[ii] This disparity has had an adverse impact on Conservative principles, figures, and ideologies. Since President Trump's inauguration, the mainstream media has published an increasingly larger number of false or erroneous stories pertaining to the President and his supporters. Some of the most prominent news stories of the past year, including the media's reporting of actor Jussie Smollett's hate crime hoax, the sexual assault allegations against Supreme Court Justice Brett Kavanaugh and the vilification of the Covington Catholic students, has helped erode the public's faith in the media to fairly and accurately report the news.

Fewer Millennials are likely to identify as conservative or vote for Republican candidates. The majority of Millennials believe that creating a fairer economy and combating climate change is more important than a limited government that creates incentives for independence and prevents undocumented immigrants from entering the country. However, more than half of

Millennials are willing to support free market principles, stronger immigration stances, and strict counterterrorism measures, so long as the proposals are not coming from President Trump or other Conservative politicians. Seventy percent of Millennials believe that the mainstream media, including the New York Times, Washington Post, CNN, ABC, CBS, and NBC has a liberal bias, yet fifty-eight percent of Millennials also believe that the mainstream media provides fair and accurate coverage of President Trump. Print and online newspapers still have a major role as a source for Millennials to receive news: Forty-four percent said that newspapers are their primary source for political news and information. However, thirty percent of Millennials receive most of their political news and information from Twitter and Facebook. That number is likely to increase in the future.

Introduction:

Core values and ideologies of Conservatism have suffered irreputable damage as a result of explicit and intentional bias that is prevalent in mainstream media outlets, including the New York Times, Washington Post, CBS, NBC, ABC and CNN. The political agenda of the mainstream media has had an adverse effect on the Conservative party, especially with younger cohorts. Millennials, particularly those with college degrees, are far more likely to identify as left wing or liberal and are more likely to vote for Democrats than to identify as Conservative and vote for Republican candidates. According to the Pew Research Center fifty seven percent of Millennials hold consistently liberal values, while just twelve percent hold consistently Conservative values.[iii] This is especially problematic for the Conservative party, since numerous studies indicate Millennials will surpass Baby Boomers in 2019 as the largest class of voters.[iv]

This book will explore clear instances of implicit bias against Conservative principles, figures, ideologies, policies, and agendas across mainstream media outlets, and how Conservatives can combat the national media onslaught that has become so pervasive and prevalent in American society that the views of a small minority of coastal elites have become normalized. It will also analyze the political attitudes of Millennials and outline strategies, tactics, and messaging that Conservatives can use to appeal to this cohort in the 2020 presidential election and in future races. If the Conservative party wishes to continue winning elections, then Conservative thought leaders must counterpunch and pushback against clear biases that have become inculcated by the mainstream media.

HYPOTHESIS:

During a 2015 Republican primary debate, Republican presidential candidate Marco Rubio remarked facetiously, "The Democrats have the ultimate super PAC, it is called the mainstream media."[v] While Rubio's statement was tongue in cheek, since President Trump has moved to 1600 Pennsylvania Avenue, the national media has turned into an arm of the Democratic party, and is willing to forego journalistic standards, ethics and norms to promulgate any narrative that is anti-Trump and supportive of the liberal agenda.

The vast majority of Millennials do not identify as Conservative, primarily due to false and arguably defamatory charges that are trumpeted through the national media, in an attempt to besmirch all things related to President Trump and Conservative principles. Due to the monopoly of left-wing ideas, these distorted and blatantly inaccurate depictions of what Conservatism truly represents, has done irreparable damage to the reputation and image of the Conservative party. With more young college educated Millennials eager to support self-described democratic socialists including Bernie Sanders and Alexandria Ocasio Cortez, it is contended that Millennials will continue to shift further to the left in the foreseeable future. However, if Millennials are not subjected to cognitive dissonance or their own preconceived notions and are presented with accurate information about the core beliefs and principles of Conservative policies, then they may not only agree with many Conservative ideologies, but may also be willing to vote for Conservatives in future elections.

RESEARCH QUESTIONS:

This book will cite examples of left-wing biases that exist in the mainstream media, including on cable news programs and traditional print media platforms, and discusses how these outlets hurt or destroy the image of Conservative leaders and ideologies. It will also look at the large percentage of journalists who identify as liberal or vote Democratic, and how this may lead to biased reporting. The paper will also address where Millennials receive their news sources from, how Millennials identify politically, and who Millennials are likely to support in the 2020 presidential election. The paper will analyze specific policies that Millennials support or are in favor of, as well as strategies, tactics, and communication messages that Conservative can leverage to counteract left-wing mainstream media bias and increase support with Millennials.

RESEARCH METHODOLOGY AND DESIGN:

The research methodology includes quantitative and qualitative research from both primary and secondary sources. The primary research consists of a survey questionnaire that identifies primary sources from which college educated Millennials receive their news and information, how they identify politically, and how traditional media influences the voting habits of Millennials. The survey seeks to identify the impact of the communication channels Millennials use to receive their news, their perceptions of media bias, the political policies that are most important to them, and the role and influence that the media plays in determining who they are likely to vote for in the 2020 presidential election. The survey was conducted using Qualtrics and sent out to fellow college and graduate students by email and through social media channels, including Facebook, LinkedIn and Twitter. The survey received 100 responses with a 10 percent plus or minus margin of error.

Secondary sources included academic studies, newspaper articles, cable news clips, research books and polls that elucidate clear instances of media biases, as well as the interests, habits and political preferences of Millennials. Academic studies, newspaper articles and cable news clips also explored what has been written and addressed on the subject of media bias.

LITERATURE REVIEW:

According to the Washington Post, only seven percent of journalists identify as Conservative or as Republicans.[vi] This disparity has adversely affected conservative principles, figures, and ideologies. The Conservative Research Media Center (RMC) noted that there are a multitude of ways that the media can spin a news story to support left wing policies. They can decide to write about a specific political topic or policy from the perspective of liberal groups, or interview liberal policy experts, while disregarding Conservative policy experts and studies done by right wing groups. They can also influence public opinion by promoting negative stories about Conservatives by placing them on the front pages of prominent newspapers, or by providing them with significant airtime on tv newscasts, while negative stories about liberals are provided much less prominence or ignored altogether.[vii]

Bernard Goldberg, a journalist who worked at CBS for twenty-eight years, articulated that "The old argument that the networks and other 'media elites' have a liberal bias is so blatantly true that its hardly worth discussing anymore. No, we don't sit around in dark corners and plan strategies on how we're going to slant the news." We don't have to. It comes naturally to most reporters."[viii] In essence, news rooms and media outlets have become echo chambers where journalists are no longer able to separate their political dispositions from simply reporting the facts, a basic requirement for objective reporting.

Goldberg concluded that two liberal newspapers, the New York Times and the Washington Post set the agenda for most network news journalists, which disproportionately leads to coverage that is overwhelmingly one sided.[ix] He also excoriated the double standard of reporters who relish the opportunity to scorn public figures, but rarely look at themselves in the mirror and admit to journalistic malfeasance when fellow journalists point out obvious biases.

> These are people who routinely stick their noses into everybody else's business. These are people who are always telling us about the media's constitutional right to investigate and scrutinize a lot of times even embarrass anyone who winds up in our crosshairs. These are people who love to take on politicians and businessmen and lawyers and Christians and the military and athletes and all sorts of other Americans, yet when one of their own writes an opinion piece about American Journalism, then you've crossed the line.[x]

The Mainstream media has had an adverse effect on the Conservative party, especially with younger cohorts. Millennials, individuals born between 1981-1996 are moving further to the left. Fifty seven percent hold consistently liberal values, while just twelve percent support Conservative values.[xi] This demographic will likely surpass Baby Boomers in 2019 as the largest class of voters. It is thus imperative for Conservatives to develop more effective communication strategies and messages if they wish to continue to win future presidential, congressional, gubernatorial, and mayoral elections.[xii]

LIMITATIONS:

A great deal has already been written about left-wing bias in the national media. Thus, the challenge for this paper is to explore and shed new light on how and why these biases occur, while also providing specific strategies, tactics and messages that Conservatives can leverage in order to more effectively appeal to Millennials in future elections. Other limitations involve ensuring that the responses to the survey questionnaire are in fact an accurate depiction of the views that Millennials share.

The primary research survey was conducted from March 19th, 2019 through April 18th, 2019 and was sent out via email. It was distributed across social media channels, including Facebook, Linkedin and Twitter. The survey had a hundred respondents, and a margin of error of plus or minus ten percentage points. Seventeen percent of respondents are not United States Citizens, but currently study or reside in the United States. More than half of the respondents are from the Northeast, and thus there is a disproportionate number of respondents from blue or liberal states. Participants were not asked to identify their race, income level, or gender.

SECONDARY RESEARCH

Mainstream media outlets including the New York Times, Washington Post, CNN, CBS, NBC, and many others purport to report news objectively. However, on reflection, consciously or unconsciously, these outlets seem predisposed to furthering leftist viewpoints by producing coverage of Conservatives that is overwhelmingly negative in nature, and often misleading due to biased reporting that omits, distorts and misrepresents pertinent information. Meanwhile, left leaning narratives and viewpoints are espoused and presented as fact, and objective journalism, but may only be an opinion.

The Conservative Research Media Center (RMC), which tracks media bias, reported that anchors, editors, producers and reporters have three major conflicts that promulgate left wing bias. The first conflict: they deny that they're liberal.[xiii] This is evidenced by the fact that only seven percent of journalists identify as Conservative or as Republicans.[xiv] The second conflict: they deny they're biased. The third conflict: they make no effort to balance their leftist worldview with Conservative viewpoints. Objective reporters do not report news in order to promote a particular political narrative, but rather, through fair and impartial reporting of facts, in which all sides are held accountable. One political party is not supposed to be favored over another in the guise of objective journalism. However, far too often, the national media reports left-leaning views and calls it news, while posing as objective journalists.

The RMC observed that there are many ways that the media

slant a news story to favor left wing policies. They may write about a specific report from the perspective of liberal groups, or interview liberal policy experts, while ignoring Conservative policy experts and studies done by Conservative groups. They can also promote negative stories about conservatives by placing them on the front pages of prominent newspapers, or by providing them with significant airtime on newscasts, while negative stories about liberals are provided much less prominence or ignored altogether.[xv]

The RMC calculated during the Bridgegate Scandal, involving former Republican governor of New Jersey Chris Christie, ABC, NBC, and CBS devoted 88 minutes of coverage to the scandal in just two days. Meanwhile, over the previous six months, those same networks spent a mere two minutes covering President Obama's targeting of conservatives by his IRS department. The RMC also noted that in 2006, when the Democrats were poised to win congressional elections and take control of the House and Senate, ABC, CBS, and NBC ran 159 stories on their evening news broadcasts, but in 2014, when Republicans were likely to retake control of the House and Senate the networks ran only 25 stories.[xvi] In other words, when there is news that is advantageous for Democrats, the media will report it, while Republicans are afforded no such luxury. Other tactics of media bias by reporters include:

> Frequently labeling conservatives with extremist tags, such as far right, or right wing, while assigning favorable labels to liberals, such as civil rights activist, or children's rights supporters. There is also bias by omission where real news is ignored if it negatively affects the liberal narrative. When all else fails, the liberal media resorts to character assassinations and personal attacks against conservatives they don't agree with.[xvii]

Bernard Goldberg, a former CBS journalist, was one of the first journalists to bring to public attention the claim that there is a left-wing bias that exists in the media, when he penned an op-ed in the Wall Street Journal in 1996 titled, *Networks Need A Reality*

Check. Goldberg subsequently wrote a book called *Bias* in which he excoriated mainstream media outlets, including The New York Times, Washington Post, CBS, NBC, and ABC for posing as objective news sources instead of an extension of the Democratic party, in which the vast majority of its staff votes for Democrats and identifies as liberal. Goldberg explained that one of the problems that allows media bias to exist is that many journalists on cable television "simply don't know what to think about certain issues until the New York Times and the Washington Post tell them what to think. Those big, important newspapers set the agenda that network news people follow."[xviii]

This is problematic because the New York Times and the Washington Post have a left-wing stance on virtually every major issue from climate change, abortion, immigration, tax reform, gun control, healthcare, housing, and education. The Times has not endorsed a Republican candidate for President since Dwight Eisenhower in 1956.[xix] Meanwhile the Washington Post has become noticeably more liberal since Jeff Bezos, the owner of Amazon purchased the newspaper in 2013. The paper even changed its slogan to *"Democracy Dies in Darkness,"* just one month after President Trump was inaugurated.[xx]

Goldberg echoed the RMC's claim by articulating that many news outlets cite "experts," to explain why a left-wing policy is beneficial in an attempt to sway public opinion and discredit right-wing policies. However, journalists and reporters often fail to disclose that these so called "experts" are often in favor of furthering left-wing policies, because they identify as liberal. This tactic was used by CBS Evening News reporter Eric Enberg, when he referred to Republican presidential candidate Steve Forbes's tax plan as a "scheme." Enberg subsequently interviewed an economist about Forbes's tax plan from the Brookings Institution without mentioning that the economist worked for a left-wing think tank and was likely to vote for Bill Clinton. Goldberg explained CBS's coverage of Forbes tax plan:

> Here's one of those dirty little secret's journalists are never supposed to reveal to the regular folks out there in the

audience: a reporter can find an expert to say anything the reporter wants, anything. Just keep calling until one of the experts says what you need him to say and tell him you'll be down with your camera crew to interview him. If you find an expert who says, "You know, I think that flat tax just might work and here's why" you thank him, hang up, and find another expert. It's how journalists sneak their own personal views into stories in the guise of objective news reporting. Because the reporter can always say, "Hey, I didn't say that flat tax stinks, the guy from that Washington think tank did!"[xxi]

Obama is standing above the country, above the world. He's sort of GOD.

The national media's primary function is to hold politicians accountable for their rhetoric and for their policies, yet there is often a noticeable imbalance or disparity between how liberal politicians and conservatives are covered. For instance, during, President Barack Obama's eight years in office, the mainstream media seldom reported on his administration's many scandals or controversies. The journalist Evan Thomas referred to President Obama as a "god." Chris Matthews of NBC said he "gets a thrill going up his leg" every time he speaks, and New York Times journalist David Brooks wrote about admiring the crease in his pants. The media wrote so glowingly of President Obama, partly to protect him, but mostly because they supported his left- wing policies and wanted to ensure that he was favorably received by the American people.[xxii] They wanted him elected president and they wanted to help ensure that he stayed at 1600 Pennsylvania Avenue for eight years. This is evidenced by the fact that at least twenty-four journalists were hired to work in President Obama's Administration, and just seven percent of journalists identify as Republican.[xxiii] The trend was no different during the 2016 presidential election, in which eighty-eight percent of journalists donated to Hillary Clinton's presidential campaign.[xxiv]

The national media had very little interest in reporting on

President Obama's weaponizing of the IRS to target Conservative not for profit groups, or his spying on Conservative journalist Ben Rosen, or his misstatements about the Affordable Care Act (ACA), in which he incorrectly claimed, on twenty-eight separate occasions that the ACA would allow patients to keep their own doctor and their healthcare plan. The media did not make a big fuss out of President Obama's cozy relationships with known left-wing radicals, race baiters, and anti-Americans including, Bill Ayers, Al Sharpton, and Reverend Jeremiah Wright, even though Ayers founded a terrorist organization that bombed government buildings and once said, "Kill all the rich people. Break up their cars and apartments. Bring the revolution home, kill your parents, that's where it's really at."[xxv] Sharpton who incited violence against Jews in Brooklyn in 1991 when he said, "If the Jews want to get it on, tell them to pin their yarmulkes back and come over to my house," was invited to the White House on over seventy occasions. [xxvi] Meanwhile, President Obama was slow to denounce Wright, even though he blamed the United States government for the September 11th attacks in a sermon where he said, "God damn America for treating our citizens as less than human. God damn America for as long as she acts like she is God and she is supreme."[xxvii]

The media was also not incensed about President Obama's knowledge of his Secretary of State Hillary Clinton's improper use of a private server,[xxviii] or his selling of the public on the Iran Nuclear Treaty, which lifted sanctions against a country whose leaders openly call for the destruction of Israel and America. Even his National Security Advisor Ben Rhodes admitted that the Obama Administration had misled naïve journalists on the details of the deal.[xxix] None of these nefarious actions seemed worthy of true investigative reporting by the mainstream media. Of course, Obama's many misdeeds would only be worthy of reporting if the media was an objective truth teller holding Democrats and Republicans equally accountable for their actions.

The national media also seldom talked about President

Obama's physical health, even though he was a lifetime smoker for more than thirty years prior to entering office and continued to smoke throughout his presidency. The national media rarely questioned why President Obama refused to draw the red line in Syria even though he had repeatedly said he would do so if Bashar al-Assad used chemical weapons against his own people. The national media hardly seemed interested in questioning why President Obama refused to refer to attacks by ISIS militants as radical Islamic extremists, even as they referred to their own atrocities in the name of Islam, and continued expanding their operation in Syria and coordinated deadly attacks in which innocent civilians were killed in cities including: New York, San Bernardino, Orlando, Paris, Brussels, Berlin, Niece, and London.[xxx]

Perhaps the greatest contrast in the media coverage between President Obama and President Trump can be found in the New York Times description of the two presidents' inauguration speeches. A Times Editorial wrote glowingly of Obama's confidence, and his ability to overcome those who doubted he was qualified to become president. They also commented on the enormous crowd size, and found space to take one last parting shot at President Bush.

> There was no shortage of powerful imagery on Barack Obama's Inauguration Day, starting with the confident man who defied all political conventions that he was too young, too inexperienced, too black or not black enough to stand on the steps of the Capitol and take the oath of office in a city and a country that are still racially divided in many shameful ways. And there was the crowd that for a day, and we hope much longer, defied those divisions. By the hundreds of thousands they came from every part of a nation that has rarely been in such peril and yet is so optimistic about its new leader. In his Inaugural Address, President Obama gave them the clarity and the respect for which all Americans have hungered. In about 20 minutes, he swept away eight years of President George Bush's false choices and failed policies and promised to recommit to America's most cherished ideals.[xxxi]

Eight years after President Obama's inauguration speech, The New York Time's was no longer impressed by an underdog story, or that of a brash New York real estate developer without any previous political experience. The Times did not mention that President Trump was the oldest president ever elected, or that he had overcome historic odds to win an election, in which the newspaper of record predicted that he had a fifteen percent chance of winning on election day. Instead of commenting on the fact that he won the electoral college by a sizeable margin, 304 compared to 227 for Hillary Clinton, or that sixty-three million people voted for him, they decided to write that he "entered office with less support in polls than any other president in recent history."

Rather than focusing on President Trump's improbable path to the White House, or the more unifying aspects of his speech, the Times chose to focus on the elements of his speech relating to aspects of America that needed fixing. These items were used as proof that his speech was gloomy and divisive, without bothering to mention that nearly every presidents' inauguration speech (including President Obama's) contrasts the hardships that Americans are currently facing, with the policies that they hope to implement to fix it. There was no mention of President Trump's proposals to help make the country stronger and more prosperous. As the Times wrote:

> Mr. Trump presented himself as the leader of a populist uprising to restore lost greatness. He outlined a dark vision of an America afflicted by "the ravages" of economic dislocation and foreign exploitation, requiring his can-do approach to turn around... Mr. Trump's view of the United States was strikingly grim for an Inaugural Address a country where mothers and children are "trapped in poverty in our inner cities," where "rusted-out factories" are "scattered like tombstones across the landscape" and where drugs and crime "have stolen too many lives... Mr. Trump assumed the presidency of a country still unsettled after a polarizing election and entered office with less support in polls than any other president in recent history... Mr. Trump made only

passing efforts to reach out to Democrats beyond thanking Mr. Obama and his wife, Michelle, for their handling of the transition.[xxxii]

The Times' assessment of President Trump's speech was deeply flawed, if not biased. The only aspects of his speech that could be characterized as dark concerned the hardships that the country was currently facing. After speaking of the carnage in the inner cities, The Times writers ignored the very next paragraph in which President Trump said: "This American carnage stops right here and stops right now. We are one nation and their pain is our pain. Their dreams are our dreams; and their success will be our success. We share one heart, one home, and one glorious destiny. The oath of office I take today is an oath of allegiance to all Americans." Surely no intellectually honest individual could characterize that as "dark" rhetoric however, the Times did not see fit to print any positive aspect of President Trump's speech. Providing credit to an individual that the media finds morally and ethically abhorrent, in favor of a political narrative, was not something the Times was interested in discussing.

The very same national media that helped elect President Obama and shied away from reporting negatively about his administration, now scrutinizes every breath President Trump takes, including how many scoops of ice cream he has for dessert. As the New York Times reported: "He lives in the White House, where he gets two scoops of ice cream instead of one for dessert. He is commander in chief, eating 'the most beautiful piece of chocolate cake' with the Chinese president while he fires missiles at Syria."[xxxiii] It was not until President Trump was elected that the New York Times suddenly became interested in the health of the Commander and Chief when they penned a headline "At 243 pounds, Trump tips the scale into obesity."[xxxiv] Instead of the media commentating on the substance of his policies and explaining which parts of his proposals are irrational they frequently resort to trivial ad hominin attacks about his personality or lack of moral character. For instance, when President Trump delivered a speech in the oval office during the government shutdown in January, in which Republicans and Democrats could not come to an agreement on border security, Gail Collins of the New York Times appeared more interested in commentating on President Trump's breathing:

> For every viewer whose response to the talk was wow we should do something about immigration. There must have been a hundred whose first reaction was why does this man keep sniffing? Deviated septum? Nasal polyps? Trump's breathing has actually sounded strange for a long time, but most of us have chosen to ignore it rather than engage in a national conversation about the president's nose. If you watched the address, and really you could have, it was only about as long as it takes to microwave popcorn you saw a 72 year old guy squinting at the teleprompter and making rather alarming breathing sounds while reading a speech about how we need a wall to protect women who are sexually assaulted on the dangerous trek up through Mexico.[xxxv]

Far too many mainstream media articles about President Trump are devoid of substance and fail to adequately address the potential merit of his policies, instead resorting to personality and character attacks. Creating an analogy between the duration of President Trump's speech and the time that it takes to microwave popcorn is no substitute for critical thinking.

Interestingly, Gail Collins failed to discuss this remark of President Trump in his speech on immigration, "America proudly welcomes millions of lawful immigrants who enrich our society and contribute to our nation. But all Americans are hurt by uncontrolled illegal migration. It strains public resources and drives down jobs and wages."[xxxvi] The media often accuses President Trump of being anti-immigration, when in reality he is merely anti-illegal immigration. One can debate whether or not illegal immigration does in fact drive down jobs and wages, but to not respond to the substance of that statement and instead comment about the President's breathing habits is substance-free lazy reporting. President Trump also cited several statistics in his speech:

> In the last two years, ICE officers made 266,000 arrests of aliens with criminal records including those charged or convicted of 100,000 assaults, 30,000 sex crimes, and 4,000 violent killings. Over the years thousands of Americans have been brutally killed by those who illegally entered our country and thousands more lives will be lost if we don't act right now. One in three women are sexually assaulted on the dangerous trek up through Mexico. Women and children are the biggest victims by far of our broken system. This is the tragic reality of illegal immigration on our southern border. This is the cycle of human suffering that I am determined to end.[xxxvii]

Gail Collins chose not to respond to the president's statement about the arrest of 266,000 aliens with criminal records, or 100,000 assaults and 4,000 violent killings. A discussion can be had as to whether or not those numbers warrant a national security crisis, but to ignore them all together, as virtually every journalist did, or to paint the numbers which were provided by Immigration Customs Enforcement (ICE), as phony or false is not only irrational, but a poor attempt at discrediting the severity of the president's remarks.

Even President Obama, a darling of the mainstream media, compared Trump to Adolph Hitler, when he spoke before the Economic Club of Chicago and said, "We have to tend to this garden of democracy or else things could fall apart quickly. That's what happened in Germany in the 1930's…sixty million people died, so you've got to pay attention. And vote." Chris Matthews of MSNBC echoed Obama's sentiment when he insisted that one of President Trump's popular slogans embraced Nazism. "America first," it was not just racial but [had] a Hitlerian background to it."[xxxviii]

Charles Blow a columnist for the New York Times, stopped just short of calling President Trump a member of the Ku Klux Klan when he wrote an article headlined, "Trump is a racist. Period." In the article, Blow said of President Trump, "It is not a stretch to say that Trump is racist. It's not a stretch to say that he is a white supremacist. It's not a stretch to say that Trump is a bigot."[xxxix] Such bellicose and truculent writing lacks anything resembling deep critical thought or journalistic standards, and has become normalized by a mainstream media that mocks all things pertaining to President Trump. One wonders whether the few conservative opinion writers in the New York Times would have been allowed to submit, unchanged anything half as damning or critical of President Obama.

President Trump's views on illegal immigration, and border security, which used to be considered mainstream in the Democratic party are now seen as xenophobic, bigoted, and immoral. In Bill Clinton's State of The Union Address 1996 he sounded eerily similar to President Trump when he instructed congress to call for more border security:

> There are some areas that the federal government must address directly and strongly. One of these is the problem of illegal immigration. After years and years of neglect, this administration has taken a strong stand to stiffen protection on our borders. We are increasing border controls by 50%; we are increasing inspections to prevent the hiring of illegal immigrants. And tonight, I announce I will sign an executive order to deny federal contracts to businesses that hire illegal immigrants. Let me be clear: we are still a nation of immigrants; we honor all those immigrants who are working hard to become new citizens. But we are also a nation of laws.[xl]

In April 1996, President Clinton signed into law the Illegal Immigration Reform and Immigrant Responsibility Act (IIRIRA), which increased penalties for unauthorized immigrants and led to higher rates of deportation. The only real difference between President Trump and President Clinton's immigration policy is that the national media never accused President Clinton of being anti-immigration.[xli]

MAINSTREAM MEDIA'S TRUMP NARRATIVE

Since President Trump was elected, the mainstream media seems focused on undermining the President and anyone associated with him. The Pew Research Center reported that during the first sixty days of President Trump's tenure, sixty-two percent of the news stories were negative, compared to just twenty percent for President Obama.[xlii] Another estimate from the Research Media Center indicated that ninety percent of the news coverage of President Trump has been negative since he took office.[xliii] This raises a question: does the reporting consist of verifiable fact, or an adversarial narrative against the President and his supporters?

One of the major national media narratives is that anyone who wears a Make America Great Again Hat (MAGA) is a member of the extreme right, with bigoted views. For instance, multiple stories that accused Trump supporters of racism, bigotry, and homophobic hate crimes turned out to be false. In many of these cases, the media, and left-wing politicians rushed to judgment before waiting for all of the facts to come out, apparently to push a narrative that would reflect poorly on President Trump and his supporters. Remarkably, once it became clear that these stories were false, the mainstream media did not show any remorse or issue adequate retractions.

In a related vein, a journalist from Time Magazine reported that a Trump staffer had removed a bust of Martin Luther King from the Oval Office when no such incident had occurred. CNN reported that Donald Trump Jr. had received advanced notice from Wiki Leaks about hacked documents that were stolen from the Democratic National Committee (DNC), when he only became aware of the documents after they were already made available to the public. ABC Reporter Brian Ross claimed that President Trump had directed his former national security advisor Michael Flynn to contact Russian Officials during the presidential race when no such conversation took place.[xliv] [xlv]

It is this "atmosphere" that accounts perhaps for the story fabricated by a gay black actor named Jussie Smollett, who claimed that he was attacked by two white men at 2AM in Chicago during a deep freeze, when people were not likely to be outside. Smollett contended that in a city where eighty-eight percent of its citizens voted for Hillary Clinton during the 2016 Presidential Election, the men shouted, "this is MAGA country," and other racist and homophobic slurs before punching him in the face, pouring bleach on him and wrapping a noose around his neck. Instead of investigating the validity of his story, the mainstream media reported it as fact.

When Smollett was interviewed on ABC by Robin Roberts, Roberts did not ask any significant follow up questions or press him on the validity of what he was saying, presumably because she was predisposed to believe that a negative story about President Trump supporters was true. Instead of asking serious questions, Roberts nodded in agreement with Smollett and asked him, "what motivated this attack...if the attackers are never found how are you able to heal?" She also provided him an opportunity for a motivational sermon when she asked what Smollett would "say to a young gay man" about overcoming homophobia.[xlvi]

Senator Corey Booker a Democrat from New Jersey and Senator Kamala Harris a Democrat from California also used the Smollett incident as an opportunity to politicize it. Booker tweeted out, "The vicious attack on actor Jussie Smollett was an attempted modern-day lynching. I'm glad he's safe."[xlvii] Harris echoed Booker's statement when she tweeted, "This was an attempted modern-day lynching. No one should have to fear for their life because of their sexuality or color of their skin. We must confront this hate."[xlviii]

Fox News reporter Tucker Carlson explained how the Smollett story fit into the media's larger narrative, "the national media long ago gave up the pretense of gathering news. Journalism is now explicitly a political job. The point of it is to enforce cultural orthodoxies and punish enemies."[xlix] The message from the media and the democrats was very clear. President Trump and his supporters are racist and hateful people. Therefore, anything that is a condemnation of the president or his supporters must be provided an endless barrage of national media coverage, even if the story itself is not true.

CASE STUDY:
FROM ADVICE AND
CONSENT TO SEARCH
AND DESTROY

In a five-month span from September 2018 through January 2019, two major anti Trump stories received a significant amount of media coverage and further exposed the biases of the mainstream media. Both stories demonstrated the extent to which the media pushes a negative narrative about the President and his supporters, risking a sacrifice of journalistic integrity. One story turned out to be entirely false; while the other story is more complicated, the media's bias in the story is straightforward.

The first story centered around Justice Brett Kavanaugh, whom Trump nominated in July to replace Justice Anthony Kennedy for the Supreme Court. Trump's announcement was immediately met with protests from left wing activists and Democrats who argued that Kavanaugh would limit abortion rights for women and take away health care from millions of Americans. After an initial round of relatively uneventful senate confirmation hearings in August, it appeared likely that Kavanaugh would be confirmed. However, in September as the senate was nearing its confirmation vote, three women came forward and accused Kavanaugh of sexual assault.

One of the women, Christine Blasey Ford accused Kavanaugh of assaulting her at a summer beach party thirty-six years ago in Montgomery County, in the summer of 1982 when she was 15. Although Ford claimed she only had one drink at the party, she could not recall virtually any significant detail of the night in question, including when the party occurred, where the house was, how she got there, or how she got home. Ford was however able to recall with what she said was 100 percent certainty that Kavanaugh had assaulted her as the Washington Post described it:

> Kavanaugh pinned her to a bed on her back and groped her over her clothes, grinding his body against hers and clumsily attempting to pull off her one-piece bathing suit and the clothing she wore over it. When she tried to scream, she said, he put his hand over her mouth. 'I thought he might inadvertently kill me. He was trying to attack me and remove my clothing.'[li]

Another woman, Deborah Ramirez, said in an interview with the New Yorker that "Kavanaugh had exposed himself at a drunken dormitory party, thrust his penis in her face, and caused her to touch it without her consent as she pushed him away. The New Yorker admitted it had "not confirmed with other eyewitnesses that Kavanaugh was present at the party. The magazine contacted several dozen classmates of Ramirez and Kavanaugh regarding the incident. Many did not respond to interview requests; others declined to comment or said they did not attend or remember the party."[li] In a startling departure from journalistic ethical standards and norms, the New Yorker decided to publish an uncorroborated claim in which not a single person could verify or confirm the validity of what Ramirez had said. It did not matter. Other media outlets reported on the same unverifiable story.

A third woman, Julie Swetnick, presented perhaps the least credible allegation against Kavanaugh. She claimed that she saw him and other Georgetown Prep classmates spike bowls of punch at parties as part of a gang rape culture. No one from those alleged parties could identify Swetnick as having been there, let alone that punch was ever served at any party. Swetnick, who would have already been in college at the time she claimed she witnessed Kavanaugh and his friends gang raping high school girls also has a history of litigation and was sued for defamation for making false statements about a former company that she worked for. Swetnick's documented lack of credibility was not enough to prevent the media from discrediting her story.

Although all three of the allegations against Kavanaugh were uncorroborated, Ford was asked to testify before Congress. Thus, her story garnered the most attention. However, Ford's story proved to be remarkably inconsistent. Every witness that Ford claimed was present denied being at the party including Leland Keyser, her best friend, who issued a statement through her lawyer under penalty of perjury, in which her attorney wrote "Simply put, Ms. Keyser does not know Mr. Kavanaugh and she has no recollection of ever being at a party or gathering where he was present, with, or without, Dr. Ford."

Perhaps the media was eager to embrace these undocumented stories because appointing Kavanaugh to the Supreme Court would dramatically shift the balance of power, as he was replacing Anthony Kennedy, who was often the swing vote in many large judicial decisions. At Kavanaugh's initial confirmation hearing, Corey Booker tried to paint him as a racist, while Kamala Harris suggested without any evidence that Kavanaugh was inappropriately working with President Trump's attorney to influence the Robert Mueller Investigation into the president's ties to Russia.

The New York Times reported in August that left-wing advocacy groups were already attempting to paint Kavanaugh as posing an "existential threat to abortion rights, the Affordable Care Act and checks on presidential power... In Washington, Democrats struggled to tar Judge Kavanaugh, a respected twelve-year veteran of the federal bench, pouring considerable energy into a fight with Republicans over access to papers from the years he worked in the White House."[lii] The media often echoed left wing talking points asserting that Kavanaugh would be a dangerous candidate for the Supreme Court, before reporting uncorroborated evidence about sexual assault allegations became a new tactic. Kavanaugh addressed this in his opening statement to

Congress, pointing out that the media and Democrats had disliked him long before he was charged with any allegations of sexual misconduct:

> Since my nomination in July, there's been a frenzy on the left to come up with something, anything to block my confirmation. Shortly after I was nominated, the Democratic Senate leader said he would "oppose me with everything he's got." A Democratic senator on this committee publicly referred to me as evil. Evil. Think about that word. And said that those that supported me were "complicit and evil." Another Democratic senator on this committee said, "Judge Kavanaugh is your worst nightmare." A former head of the Democratic National Committee said, "Judge Kavanaugh will threaten the lives of millions of Americans for decades to come.[liii]

After the hearing, in which Ford and Kavanaugh both provided compelling testimony, the New York Times made no secret of who it thought was the more credible witness and ought to be believed:

> Judge Kavanaugh, who bristled with red-faced outrage and grievance at what he called an orchestrated campaign to destroy his life…In contrast, Dr. Blasey bolstered her credibility not only by describing in harrowing detail what she did remember, but by being honest about what she didn't, like the exact date of the gathering, or the address of the house where it occurred. As she pointed out, the precise details of a trauma get burned into the brain and stay there long after less relevant details fade away. She came across as Everywoman an Everywoman with a Ph.D. at once guileless about politics yet schooled in the science of memory and psychology, "terrified," as she put it, to be at the center of the vortex.[liv]

The New York Times failed to explain why outrage towards thirty-six-year-old uncorroborated allegations that accused Kavanaugh of sexual assault and gang rape and a sterling judicial reputation that was destroyed in a matter of days by the mainstream media rendered him a non-credible witness. Although Ford was unable to recall virtually any important detail of information about the event in question, according to the Times, she was the more reliable witness because she was able to explain the workings of the brain and why she could remember some pieces of information and not others. In other words, if an individual has a Ph.D. in psychology and understands why she cannot recall crucial bits of information when making serious allegations against a man with a clean record, the important element is not that the individual cannot recall the information, but that the individual can explain why they cannot recall it.

As it became clearer that Ford's story had multiple inconsistencies, the media chose to echo the talking points of Democratic senators by focusing on Kavanaugh's demeanor, his facial expressions, and whether or not he was lying about his drinking habits. Whether or not he was actually guilty of committing sexual misconduct thirty-six years earlier became secondary. The Democratic senators couldn't prove that Kavanaugh had in fact assaulted Ford, so they instead painted him as an alcoholic by asking him to decipher references from his high school year book that would at the very least prove that he was an irresponsible teenager. As Democratic Senator of Rhode Island Sheldon Whitehouse said to Kavanaugh during one exchange at the hearing, "Let's look at 'Beach Week Ralph Club Biggest Contributor,' what does the word Ralph mean in that?... So, the vomiting that you reference in the Ralph Club reference, related to the consumption of alcohol?"[lv] Jonah Goldberg of National Review described the absurdity:

> Print publications are flooding the zone to get to the bottom of Boofgate and Ice-Throw-Gotterdammerung. As if proving that a yearbook quote meant some other juvenile thing, or that if he threw some ice cubes in a bar tussle, that would prove . . . something. Kavanaugh, fully aware that he will get no benefit of any doubt, offers lawyerly and arguable evasive answers mostly about trivialities and, like a self-fulfilling prophecy, these ambiguous answers are taken as proof of perjury and drunken perfidy that the press must get to the bottom of.[lvi]

According to Democrats and the media, even if Kavanaugh

did not assault Ford, showing too much emotion and providing evasive answers to questions about drinking references from his high school year book page were seen as disqualifying from serving on the Supreme Court. [lvii] Don Lemon of CNN claimed that there were "serious questions about the veracity of Brett Kavanaugh's claims about drinking under oath. How much he drank, and how regularly and whether he could have had blackouts from his drinking."[lviii] Lemon's colleague, Chris Cuomo said of Kavanaugh's testimony at the hearing, "We have never seen such an overtly political play by a nominee...when you're innocent, poise, calm in the face of criticism reflect your power of belief. Losing control suggests something incriminating. Kavanaugh is who he was in that hearing."[lix] In other words, Kavanaugh's anger at what he believes were false allegations about him prove that he's guilty. Gesticulating and raising one's voice confirmed that Kavanaugh assaulted Ford. Jonah Goldberg elucidated on the media's one-sided coverage of Kavanaugh:

> Whole panels of pundits and experts on MSNBC are made up of people who cannot imagine why Kavanaugh might be upset at the unverified, uncorroborated, and literally unbelievable claim that he ran a rape gang when he was 15. Instead, we get hours of hand-wringing every day about his supposedly unjudicial temperament, as if any judge or justice on the bench, now or ever, would be expected to remain calm under such circumstances...

Goldberg contended that so called objective journalists should:

> Care every bit as much about disproving the allegations of Swetnick, Ramirez, and yes Ford as proving them. Your job as you've said countless times, preening in your heroic martyr status in the age of Trump is to report the facts. If Swetnick is lying, you should want to report that every bit as much as you would if you could prove that Kavanaugh is. Because you're not supposed to have a team.[lx]

A few days after the hearing, 86-year-old Democratic Senator Diane Feinstein of California attempted to portray Kavanaugh as that of an unhinged man who had no business serving on the highest court. "We saw a man filled with anger and aggression. Judge Kavanaugh raised his voice, he interrupted senators...this behavior revealed a hostility and belligerence that is unbecoming of someone seeking to be elevated to the United States Supreme Court."[lxi] One could be forgiven for forgetting that Kavanaugh was initially accused of assaulting women, not of being "filled with anger and aggression." Character attacks about Kavanaugh's anger and temperament became new talking points for the Democrats to disqualify him from the Supreme Court, and the media was more than happy to play along.

While Ford should be praised for coming forward with her story, there were many holes in it that were observed by Rachel Mitchell, the prosecutor who questioned Ford at the hearing. Mitchell who has been a sex crimes prosecutor for 25 years released a memo in which she summarized her findings about the hearing:

> In the legal context, here is my bottom line: A "he said, she said" case is incredibly difficult to prove. But this case is even weaker than that. Dr. Ford identified other witnesses to the event, and those witnesses either refuted her allegations or failed to corroborate them. I do not think that a reasonable prosecutor would bring this case based on the evidence before the Committee. Nor do I believe that this evidence is sufficient to satisfy the preponderance of the evidence standard.[lxii]

A New York Times editorial admonished the male Republican senators for refusing to question Ford, even though in all likelihood, the media would have characterized them as a group of sexist men who were attempting to cross examine a supposed victim of sexual assault. In case any viewer of the hearing had the impression that Mitchell had done an effective job of examining Ford's many inconsistencies or lack of compelling evidence against Kavanaugh, the Times editorial left no doubt that Mitchell had not in fact raised any series questions into Ford's allegations:

> Perhaps the most maddening part of Thursday's hearing was the cowardice of the committee's 11 Republicans, all of them men, and none of them, apparently, capable of asking Dr. Blasey a single question. They farmed that task out to a sex-crimes prosecutor named Rachel Mitchell, who tried unsuccessfully in five-minute increments to poke holes in Dr. Blasey's story.[lxiii]

One wonders if the Times journalists noticed any discrepancies in Ford's story. As Mitchell pointed out in the memo, Ford had no memory of the key details of the night in question. Ford could not remember who invited her to the party, how she got to the party, where the house was located or how she left the party. Perhaps most importantly from the memo, Mitchell wrote that "Dr. Ford's account of the alleged assault has not been corroborated by anyone she identified as having attended (the party) including her lifelong friend."[lxiv]

As it became clearer that Ford's story was unlikely to prevent Kavanaugh from receiving the nomination, the Times did their best to undermine him in other ways, by echoing Democratic talking points and stipulating that Ford was polite to the senators, while Kavanaugh was abrasive and clearly did not have the temperament required of a supreme court justice:

> What a study in contrasts: Where Christine Blasey Ford was calm and dignified, Brett Kavanaugh was volatile and belligerent; where she was eager to respond fully to every questioner, and kept worrying whether she was being "helpful" enough, he was openly contemptuous of several senators; most important, where she was credible and unshakable at every point in her testimony, he was at some points evasive, and some of his answers strained credulity.[lxv]

While there was certainly a contrast in tone and demeanor between Ford and Kavanaugh, there was also a contrast in the senators' treatment of them. Every single Democratic senator (including Rachel Michell) was sympathetic and polite to Ford, as they should have been. They allowed her to answer their questions on her own terms without interrupting her. Meanwhile when it became Kavanaugh's turn to answer questions from the democratic senators, their tone shifted dramatically. Kavanaugh was treated as though he was unequivocally guilty of Ford's allegations, and the onus was squarely on him to prove that he was innocent.

The New York Times did not analyze why Kavanaugh was forced to defend himself against a barrage of baseless allegations that destroyed his name and reputation. One wonders if Democratic senators and the editorial board at the New York Times would have covered Kavanaugh in the same way if he were nominated by President Obama. Would they have vilified him if he displayed strong emotions towards partisan senators who accused him of allegations of sexual assault based on the flimsiest of evidence? Would they have decried his outrage as proof of his guilt? Would they write that the senator "was volatile and belligerent" or would they characterize his anger as justified?

It is certainly true that Kavanaugh did not handle himself particularly well in certain instances throughout the hearing. Most notably, when responding to questioning from Amy Klobuchar, the Democratic Senator from Minnesota who asked him if he had ever blacked out before, he responded by saying, "I don't know have you?" It was a rude and insulting remark, one that Kavanaugh deeply regretted as he later apologized to Klobuchar during the hearing. Kavanaugh also wrote an op-ed in the Wall Street Journal in which he explained why he was so emotional at the hearing:

> My hearing testimony was forceful and passionate. That is because I forcefully and passionately denied the allegation against me. At times, my testimony both in my opening statement and in response to questions reflected my overwhelming frustration at being wrongly accused, without corroboration, of horrible conduct completely contrary to my record and character... I was very emotional last Thursday, more so than I have ever been. I might have been too emotional at times. I know that my tone was sharp, and I said

a few things I should not have said.[lxvi]

Perhaps the most logical explanation as to why Kavanaugh was eventually confirmed was summarized by republican Senator Susan Collins of Maine, who explained why she would vote to confirm Kavanaugh. "The facts presented do not mean that professor Ford was not sexually assaulted that night or at some other time. But they do lead me to conclude that the allegations fail to meet the more likely than not standard. Therefore, I do not believe that these charges can fairly prevent Judge Kavanaugh from serving on the court."[lxvii]

Although Brett Kavanaugh was eventually confirmed to the Supreme Court, Kevin Williamson a writer for the National Review summarized the intertwining philosophy of the Democrats and the mainstream media:

> The Democrats' strategy can be summarized: "Sure, you may win an election. And, sure, you may be an accomplished jurist with a sterling record. But if you come between us and what we want and what we want is the power to dominate you then we will slander you as a rapist, and our media friends will see to it that this slander, no matter how obviously false, is the first thing people think about when they think about you, for the rest of your life. You may beat us in an election, but we'll take it out on your children, and we have the New York Times and the Yale Law School.

CASE STUDY: THERE'S SOMETHING AGGRESSIVE ABOUT STANDING THERE

The second major news story of anti- President Trump media bias occurred in January after a four-minute video of predominately white students from Covington High School, an all-boys Catholic school in Kentucky went viral. The video appeared to show boys who were wearing Make America Great Again (MAGA) hats doing the tomahawk chop and mocking a 64-year old Native American man named Nathan Phillips, who claimed he was a former Vietnam War veteran. At the onset, the students who were in Washington D.C. for a pro-life rally, had very little sympathy from the media. They were white Catholic boys, wearing MAGA hats, in town to celebrate the life of children whose mothers chose not to have an abortion.

According to the Washington Post, Philips claimed that he was trying to get to the top steps of the Lincoln Memorial before the Covington students mobbed him and began chanting "build that wall," a reference to President Trump's campaign promise to build a wall along the southern border to keep out undocumented immigrants. Philips also told the Post that he felt threatened by the teens and that they swarmed him as he and other activists were wrapping up (the Indigenous People's March) and preparing to leave. The vilification of the Covington boys by the mainstream media commenced within mere hours of the video's release from an unverified account on Twitter.

One of the Covington students shown in the video was a white sixteen-year old named Nick Sandmann who was seen wearing a MAGA hat and smirking mere inches from Philips face. Over the next twenty-four hours, the interaction between Sandmann and Philips played on an endless loop by virtually all of the major cable networks and was front page news. Politicians, journalists, and pundits all chimed in to denounce Sandmann as a racist and bigoted white boy who used his smirk to exert his privilege and dominance over an elderly Native American. Ruth Graham of Slate, compared Sandmann's smirk to that of a group of racist southerners during the Civil Rights Movement in the 1960's:

> The face is both punchable and untouchable. The face is in this photo of a clutch of white young men crowding around a single black man at a lunch counter sit-in in Virginia in the 1960s, and in many other images of jeering white men from that era. . . .Anyone who knew the popular white boys in high school recognized it: the confident gaze, the eyes twinkling with menace, the smirk. The face of a boy who is not as smart as he thinks he is, but is exactly as powerful. The face that sneers, "What? I'm just standing here," if you flinch or cry or lash out. The face knows that no matter how you react, it wins.[lxviii]

The New York Times wrote a headline about the incident titled, "Boys in 'Make America Great Again' Hats Mob Native Elder at Indigenous Peoples March" and another Times headline read, "A throng of cheering and jeering high school boys" were "surrounding a Native American elder."[lxix] Ilhan Omar, the Democratic congresswoman from Minnesota tweeted to her 611,000 followers that the Covington boys were "taunting 5 black men before they surrounded Phillips and led racist chants."[lxx] Rezla Aslan an author and tv host tweeted about Nick Sandmann, "Honest question. Have you ever seen a more punchable face than this kid's?"[lxxi] One journalist who was later fired for wishing death on the students tweeted, "I don't know what it says about me, but I've truly lost the ability to articulate the hysterical, nausea, and heartache this makes me feel. I just want these people to die. Simple as that. Every single one of them. And their parents."[lxxii]

The only problem with the media's reporting about the incident was that none of it was true. A longer video of the incident was later released which refuted most of the claims that Phillips made to the Washington Post, CNN, and NBC. All of these outlets reported virtually every statement that Phillips had made about the incident as though it were fact, without verifying it with any other sources. The full-length video not only absolved the Covington kids of any wrongdoing, but also revealed that they themselves were subjected to verbal abuse by four people who identified as Hebrew Israelites, a fringe group that believes there are 12 tribes chosen by god and does not consider white people among those tribes.[lxxiii]

The full video revealed that the incident started when the Hebrew Israelites began yelling at a group of Native Americans who were there for there the Indigenous Peoples March. The Israelites shouted derogatory remarks including, "Indian means savage" and referred to one of the Native Americans as a "damn uncle tomahawk." The Covington boys who were waiting for their bus to take them back to Kentucky were curious as to what the Israelites were saying and so they moved closer to listen. Members of the Israelites noticed the students and then began shouting racial epithets at them, including: "You little dirty ass crackers, your day coming...On the back of your dollar bill, it says in god we trust, but you give faggots rights...This is a bunch of future school shooters...The biggest terrorist on the face of the earth is the pale face man, woman and child." The Israelites even made a reference to the film *Get Out* when they said to one of the black students from Covington, "When you get old enough, they're gonna steal your organs," and they referred to the kids as "a bunch of Donald Trump incest children."[lxxiv]

As the Israelites continued shouting epithets at the Covington students, the students received permission from their teachers to perform one of their school spirit chants commonly used at sporting events to drown out the noise of the Israelites. It was at that moment that video evidence clearly shows Philips approaching the students from one end of the Lincoln Memorial, with a drum in his hand. Philips inserted himself directly into the group of Covington students, and planted his feet in front of Sandmann. He did not make any effort to get to the top of Lincoln Memorial as he had previously claimed in countless interviews including one with NBC, in which he said of the students, "they surrounded us, and that's when I realized the dangerous situation I was in. I couldn't go left, I couldn't go right, we couldn't go back without running into this mob."[lxxv] Philips then said of Sandmann, "When that young man blocked my retreat, he put himself in front of me." As the media continued to smear Sandmann and the Covington students, Sandmann released a statement defending himself and refuted Philips version of the event:

> At no time did I hear any student chant anything other than the school spirit chants. I did not witness or hear any students chant "build that wall" or anything hateful or racist at any time. Assertions to the contrary are simply false. Our chants were loud because we wanted to drown out the hateful comments that were being shouted at us by the protestors. After a few minutes of chanting, the Native American protestors, who I hadn't previously noticed, approached our group. The Native American protestors had drums and were accompanied by at least one person with a camera. The protestor everyone has seen in the video began playing his drum as he waded into the crowd, which parted for him. I did not see anyone try to block his path. He locked eyes with me and approached me, coming within inches of my face. He played his drum the entire time he was in my face. I never interacted with this protestor. I did not speak to him. I did not make any hand gestures or other aggressive moves... I never felt like I was blocking the Native American protestor. He did not make any attempt to go around me. It was clear to me that he had singled me out for a confrontation, although I am not sure why. The engagement ended when one of our teachers told me the busses had arrived and it was time to go.[lxxvi]

Every word from Sandmann's statement was confirmed by the full-length video of the incident. Yet the mainstream media did not issue an apology to Sandmann and the rest of the Covington students. One CNN video that had falsely accused Sandmann of mocking and threatening Philips was scrubbed from the internet, as if it had never existed. A Washington Post Headline read, "The mainstream media rushed to keep up. The Trump internet pounced." The real narrative was not that the media enabled a false story about a group of white male catholic students who were now receiving death threats, but rather that Trump supporters were angry at how the media falsely portrayed the Covington students. The journalists were now the victims because they simply could not keep up with the speed of social media.

Sandmann's family is now suing both CNN and the Washington Post for $525 million in punitive damages for their libelous coverage of him.[lxxvii] [lxxviii] As Sandmann's attorney said of the media's failure to exercise the most basic forms of journalistic integrity, "without any reasonable investigation, they took something straight off Twitter that had been in essence manipulated so that it told one story and they reported it as the truth." Perhaps even more remarkably, even after the full-length videos revealed that Phillips had fabricated virtually everything that he said about the incident, he was still granted numerous interviews in which the media continued to portray him as a victim.

Both Philips and Sandmann were interviewed by Savannah Guthrie on NBC's Today Show, yet the disparity in how they were treated was palpable. Sandmann who received multiple death threats was asked questions by Guthrie that included, "Do you feel from this experience, that you owe anybody an apology? Do you see your own fault? Have you looked at that video and thought about how it felt from the others perspective? In other words, there were a lot of you, a handful of the others, do you think they might have felt threatened by a bunch of young men kind of beating their chests? Do you think if you weren't wearing that hat, this might not have happened, or it might have been different?"[lxxix]

Even as the questions became more nonsensical and inappropriately aggressive, Sandmann answered each question calmly and with poise. With Guthrie seemingly unable to unnerve Sandmann or bait him into losing his cool, for good measure she added, "There's something aggressive about standing there, standing your ground." Guthrie failed to ask Sandmann if he felt threatened by the racial epithets that were hailed in his direction by the Israelites, or by Philips, an adult who decided to walk up to him and bang a drum mere inches from his face. She also failed to ask him if he felt that he was owed an apology by members of the news media, or by Philips for all of the blatant lies that had been reported and written about him.[lxxx]

The national media's takeaway from Sandmann's interview was that he showed no remorse for his actions and did not believe that he owed Philips an apology. That was the headline that several national news organizations decided to run with. Eddie Glaude, a contributor to MSNBC wondered why Sandmann was even allowed to be interviewed when he said, "there was this attempt to kind of give a fuller account of the young man…we give privilege to these white kids. He can sit down with Savanna Guthrie and redeem himself, but then there's all of these other folk(s) who we just presume aren't so innocent." Why Sandmann should not have been allowed to defend himself, given that he had received death threats for merely standing in place with a nervous grin on his face was not something that the national media was interested in discussing. No one bothered to ask why Sandmann owed an apology to Philips, as Kyle Smith of National Review wrote:

> If you're in a public place and someone starts heckling you, are you entitled to heckle back? How about if someone does something much worse than heckling you in a public place? What if that person in fact takes a drum up to you and starts banging it in your face? Are you entitled to heckle back? How about smirking? Are you allowed to smirk?[lxxxi]

Tucker Carlson of Fox News, said sardonically of Guthrie's

interview with Sandmann, "Failing to move is a hostile act. We can't have people standing still in public places." Carlson compared the medias attacks on Sandmann to the equivalent of what the author George Orwell called "Facecrime." In his novel *1984*, Orwell wrote, "To wear an improper expression on your face was itself a punishable offense. There was even a word for it Facecrime."

By the time Guthrie interviewed Philips, her tone shifted dramatically from one of finger pointing towards one of empathy. Guthrie's line of questioning mirrored that of the Jussie Smollett interview with Robin Roberts, in which she asked Phillips, "How are you doing and how are you feeling?" She asked Phillips if he felt threatened, and what he hoped the cultural lesson for this incident would be.

The trends are not difficult to pick up on. Jussie Smollett, Chrtine Ford, and Nathan Philips were all anti-Trump and anti-conservative and so the sympathetic media allowed them to share their version of the truth on their own turns and without any pushback. On the other hand, the responsibility was left solely with Brett Kavanaugh, and Nick Sandmann to explain why they were not guilty of the most heinous of crimes, sexual assault and racial insensitivity.

Guthrie's did not ask Philips why he blatantly lied about walking over to Sandmann and started pounding a drum in his face. She did not question him as he continued to falsely accuse the Covington kids of threatening the Israelites and showing anger towards them. She did not attempt to refute what everyone knew was a lie when he maintained his stance that Sandmann had "surrounded him." She did not ask him why he thought that "there was a lack of responsibility," or "sincerity" from Sandmann in his public comments about the incident. She did however, allow Philips to maintain his stance that he heard the kids chant "build the wall," even though the only video evidence of anyone chanting "build the wall" came from the black Israelites.

When Guthrie's asked Philips if he thought he should have walked away Philips said, "that's what I was trying to do. I was trying to walk away...we were surrounded." Guthrie did not attempt to refute that, even though the producers at NBC could have played the video of Philips inserting himself into the Covington crowd and asked him to explain why his rhetoric did not match what our own eyes were telling us. If there was one bright spot for Guthrie, it was when she softly questioned Philips about his military service, in which he had falsely claimed that he had served in Vietnam.[lxxxii] The unspoken message from the mainstream media was very clear on both Brett Kavanaugh and the Covington incidents: anyone who supports President Trump or those who are appointed to serve on the Supreme Court by the President ought not to be believed, because anyone who is affiliated with him is fostering a hateful ideology. Kyle Smith also noted the parallel between George Orwell's *1984* and Nick Sandmann:

> The Left started out incensed that the Covington kids were wearing hats and smiles, and now that we know those kids didn't "mob" or "surround" a Native American but simply jeered a bit in response to an obnoxious activist who entered their group and pounded a drum in their faces, we're back to the original charges: hatecrime and facecrime.[lxxxiii]

It is striking that while the media fact checks every single word that President Trump says, the media does not correct itself when it covers a story incorrectly. Journalistic standards of integrity, and norms cannot be brushed aside, when an individual reporter or member of a particular media outlet or group is covering a President or supporters whose political views do not align with their own. As the Conservative political commentator Mark Levin said when considering the news stories that have circulated during President Trump's tenure:

> Poll after poll, survey after survey shows that the media are liberal and democrat. We have a packed media with a groupthink mentality. There are no uniform binding standards among news outlets. No clear line between news and opinion. No universal rules of professional conduct that apply to doctors and lawyers, and electricians and plumbers. No commitment to objectivity. No commitment to truth telling. There is all this old-fashioned yellow journalism. Scandal-

ous, sensational, intellectually corrupt...The mass media in this country, were committed to Hillary Clinton's election, now they're committed to ousting Donald Trump, every single day. They're sloppy, they miss report, they don't care, and they figure they'll throw out an apology if they must. They try to destroy the president, his family, and anybody associated with him, his staff, Kavanaugh, anything. They have never treated liberal democrats this way.[lxxxiv]

PRIMARY RESEARCH

A primary research survey on mainstream media's political bias was conducted from March 19th, 2019 through April 18, 2019 using Qualtrics software. The survey consisted of a questionnaire that identified where college educated Millennials receive their news and information from, how they identify politically, and whether traditional and social media outlets influence the voting habits of Millennials. The survey also sought to measure the impact of the communication channels Millennials use to receive their news, their perceptions of media bias, and the political policies that are most important to them.

In the survey, nearly half of all respondents or forty-four percent of Millennials listed print or online newspapers as their primary communication channel for receiving their political news and information, while thirty one percent of respondents listed social media (including Twitter and Facebook) as their second most frequent communication channel for receiving political news. Just twelve percent of Millennials listed cable news programs as their primary source for political news and information.

Exactly half of all Millennials identified themselves as liberal or Democrat, while just seventeen percent identified as conservative or Republican. Fourteen percent of respondents did not identify with any political party, eight percent identified as independent, and four percent identified as socialist. Seventy-seven percent of Millennials said that they were either unlikely or extremely unlikely to vote for President Trump in 2020, while just thirteen percent said that they were either extremely likely or somewhat likely to vote for him. Seventy two percent of Millennials also said they were most likely to vote for a democrat in the

2020 election, while just fifteen percent said they were likely to vote for a republican, and seven percent said they would not vote. Nearly half of all respondents or forty eight percent said that factors other than social media and friends and family would have the biggest influence on the candidate that they decide to vote for in the 2020 election.

Fifty six percent of Millennials disagreed with the statement that their views are mostly shaped by the news media, while twenty seven percent agreed that the media plays a dominant role in shaping their views. Nearly half of all respondents, or forty six percent said that friends and family had the largest influence on their political views, while twenty one percent said social media had the most significant impact on their political views.

Nearly three fourths of all Millennials or seventy two percent agreed that the mainstream media including the New York Times, Washington Post, CNN, ABC, CBS, and NBC has a liberal bias, while just fourteen percent disagreed. Thirty five percent of all respondents listed the left leaning New York Times as their preferred media outlet, while just fifteen percent listed the right leaning Wall Street Journal as their preferred outlet. Fourteen percent listed social media as their preferred media outlet. Nearly half of all Millennials or forty nine percent believe that the mainstream media provides fair and accurate coverage of President Donald Trump, while just twenty seven percent disagreed with that assessment.

In one question, the respondents were provided a combination of conservative and liberal policies and were asked to rank them in importance. Forty eight percent of all respondents believed that creating an economy that works for all, not just the very wealthy, was most important to them. Thirty one percent believed climate change is an urgent threat and a defining challenge of our time. Just six percent of participants believe that limited government is a necessary evil required to maintain a civil society, and only six percent thought that policies are only as useful as the incentives they create, not the good intentions with which they were created. Only two percent believed that those who cross the

U.S. border illegally should be detained by Immigration and Customs Enforcement (ICE) and subjected for deportation.

Exactly half of all Millennials agreed with the statement by the free market economist Milton Friedman, who said "The great virtue of a free market system is that it does not care what color people are; it does not care what their religion is; it only cares whether they can produce something you want to buy. It is the most effective system we have discovered to enable people who hate one another to deal with one another and help one another." Forty percent also agreed with an anti-capitalism quote by democratic congresswoman Alexandria Ocasio Cortez, who said that "Capitalism is an ideology of capital, the most important thing is the concentration of capital and to seek and maximize profit. And that comes at any cost to people and to the environment, so to me capitalism is irredeemable." Thirty three percent of respondents disagreed with Cortez's statement.

Participants were also asked to identify the speaker of an immigration policy that Bill Clinton delivered during a state of the union address in 1996, in which he said:

> There are some areas that the federal government must address directly and strongly. One of these is the problem of illegal immigration. After years and years of neglect, this administration has taken a strong stand to stiffen protection on our borders. We are increasing border controls by 50%; we are increasing inspections to prevent the hiring of illegal immigrants. And tonight, I announce I will sign an executive order to deny federal contracts to businesses that hire illegal immigrants. Let me be clear: we are still a nation of immigrants; we honor all those immigrants who are working hard to become new citizens. But we are also a nation of laws.

Forty-two percent of respondents incorrectly identified Barack Obama as the speaker, while thirty two percent were able to correctly identify Bill Clinton as the speaker. Thirteen percent believed Donald Trump was the speaker and eleven percent thought George W. Bush was the speaker. Nearly half of all respondents or forty nine percent agreed with Bill Clinton's immigration stance, while roughly one quarter of respondents or twenty one percent disagreed.

Seventy seven percent of participants agreed with an anonymous quote that Barack Obama made regarding his foreign policy strategy, in which he said, "I have made it clear that we will hunt down terrorists who threaten our country, wherever they are. That means I will not hesitate to take action against ISIL in Syria, as well as Iraq. This is a core principle of my presidency: if you threaten America, you will find no safe haven." Only eleven percent of respondents disagreed.

WHERE DO MILLENNIALS STAND?

There are several major takeaways from the survey. Print and online newspapers are still a major source for Millennials to receive their news from, as is evidenced by the forty-four percent of respondents who said that print and online newspapers are where they receive the majority of their political news and information. However, social media was a close second, with thirty percent of Millennials indicating that they receive most of their political news and information from Twitter and Facebook. That number is likely to continue to rise in the near future, as social media continues to grow as a source for where Millennials receive their political news from.

It was not surprising that fifty percent of Millennials identified themselves as either liberal or Democrat, while just seventeen percent identified themselves as Conservative or Republican. Fifty-five percent of Millennials disagreed with the assessment that their views are mostly shaped by the news media. This somewhat disproves part of the hypothesis of this paper, which is that there are fewer Millennials who identify as Conservative, primarily due to liberal mainstream media bias. The lack of influence on the views of Millennials from the news media can be attributed to the fact that forty five percent of Millennials believed that friends and family had the largest impact on their political views. This rings true: political beliefs and attitudes of Millennials were probably shaped by friends and family, long before they started consuming the news. It was somewhat surprising to learn that social and traditional media only impacted the views of Millennials by twenty one percent, given that traditional media remains the most dominant source of news for Millennials, and given the amount of time that Millennials spend on social media.

Seventy percent of Millennials believe that the mainstream media, including the New York Times, Washington Post, CNN, ABC, CBS, and NBC has a liberal bias, yet fifty eight percent of Millennials believe that the mainstream media provides fair and accurate coverage of President Trump. Perhaps Millennials are willing to acknowledge that the mainstream media is biased, but they also believe that President Trump's behavior and rhetoric has warranted the coverage that he received from the media. It is also possible that many Millennials have not been reading the New York Times or Washington Post for the last two years, or have not watched CNN and MSNBC's endless barrage of coverage accusing President Trump of colluding with the Russian government during the 2016 presidential election.

Forty four percent of Millennials said that they receive most of their political news and information from print or online newspapers. Although thirty five percent of Millennials said that the New York Times was their preferred media outlet, only fifteen percent said they receive their news from the Wall Street Journal. Twenty seven percent said that they prefer other media outlets over the New York Times, Wall Street Journal, Washington Post, Huffington Post and social media. Thus, it is likely that other online sites such as Politico, the Drudge Report, the Hill, Salon, or Breitbart are more prominent news sources for Millennials to receive their political news and information from. Podcasts, which have increased in popularity in the last several years may also be a common place for Millennials to receive their political news and information.

Unsurprisingly seventy two percent of Millennials said that they were likely to vote Democratic in the next election and seventy six percent said they were either unlikely or extremely unlikely to vote for President Trump in the 2020 election. The data clearly illustrates that even Millennials who do not consider themselves a member of the Democratic Party, overwhelmingly prefer to vote Democrat than Republican. Forty nine percent of Millennials also did not have a clear sense of who or what would have the biggest influence on determining the candidate that they decide to vote for in the 2020 election. In other words, the majority of Millennials believe that most of the places where they receive their political news and information from including: friends, family and traditional/ social media will not have a large impact on who they choose to vote for in the upcoming presidential election.

Since more Millennials are embracing anti- capitalist and socialist ideologies, it was somewhat surprising to learn that fifty percent of Millennials agreed with a pro capitalist and free market statement from the economist Milton Friedman. That number seemed especially high considering that thirty nine percent of Millennials also said that they agreed with a quote by Democrat Congresswoman Alexandria Ocasio Cortez, in which she said that "capitalism is irredeemable."

When Millennials were asked to rank statements that were most important to them, it was not surprising that creating a fairer economy and climate change were amongst their most important concerns. Increasing taxes on the wealthy or top one percent of income earners, as well as focusing on combating climate change have long been Democrat talking points in the last several election cycles. Deporting undocumented immigrants or having concerns about the economic impact on allowing more immigrants to enter the country illegally, as well as creating policies that have incentives for productivity and independence as opposed to merely good intentions were considered least important to Millennials.

Forty-two percent of participants believed that Bill Clinton's immigration policy, was actually Barack Obama's, and sixty four percent of Millennials agreed with his statement. This was pretty surprising, considering that President Trump's immigration policy has echoed many themes of President Clinton's, specifically, in terms of not rewarding people for breaking the law, as well as illegal immigration having serious economic implications on the

U.S economy.

Fifty five percent of respondents agreed with President Obama's anonymous statement that also had traces of President Trump's basic foreign policy stance, "If you threaten America, you will find no safe haven." While the respondents might not have specifically known that the speaker was President Obama, likely they did not believe that it was President Trump. President Obama notably referred to "ISIS" as "ISIL," and the rhetorical elements of the statement were more thorough, organized, and articulate than those of President Trump who once said of his immigration policy, "Donald J. Trump is calling for a total and complete shutdown of Muslims entering the United States until our country's representatives can figure out what the hell is going on."[lxxxv]

Much of the conclusions that are reached from the survey questionnaire confirms the hypothesis of this paper, that many Millennials' views are motivated by the individual espousing a particular position and not necessarily by whether or not they agree with the specific policy proposal. In other words, Millennials (and most humans for that matter) will essentially base their opinion or a particular viewpoint, depending on whether or not they agree or like the speaker. They simply ignore the resulting "cognitive dissonance" or inconsistency in their views.

In other words, there have been instances where President Trump has mirrored both Bill Clinton and Barack Obama in terms of his political stances and policies. Yet Millennials have a much more positive image of President Clinton and President Obama then they do of President Trump, therefore they are likely to discredit most if not all that President Trump says, even if a specific statement is similar to those of past presidents that they supported.

HOW CONSERVATIVES CAN APPEAL TO MILLENNIALS

If Conservatives wish to appeal to Millennial voters, they must strike a balance between a softer and more compassionate tone, while also emphasizing liberty, limited government, personal responsibility and principles that the country's founding father Thomas Jefferson laid out in the Declaration of Independence. Conservatives can acknowledge the past evils that plagued this country, including slavery, segregation, Jim Crow laws, and gender discrimination, while also reminding Millennials that this country remains the freest in the world and was founded on the premise that we are all endowed by our creator, "with certain unalienable Rights, that among these are Life, Liberty and the pursuit of Happiness."[lxxxvi]

The Heritage Foundation believes that there are six important Conservative principles including, god free will, and "the right to be free from the restrictions of arbitrary force." The idea that "liberty is indivisible, and that political freedom cannot long exist without economic freedom." The principle that "the purpose of government is to protect those freedoms through the preservation of internal order, the provision of national defense, and the administration of justice." The Constitution, while not flawless, remains "the best arrangement yet devised for empowering government to fulfill its proper role, while restraining it from the concentration and abuse of power." The ideas that capitalism remains the greatest enhancer at lifting people out of poverty and that, "the free play of supply and demand, is the single economic system compatible with the requirements of personal freedom and constitutional government; and that it is at the same time the most productive supplier of human needs." Finally, Millennials should be reminded that America's foreign policy must always be looked at from the viewpoint of whether or not it serves "the just interests of the United States."[lxxxvii]

Conservative leaders should remind Millennials that focusing on intersectionality, or the idea that there are varying levels of victimization dependent on race, class and gender is detrimental to their success. It is certainly beyond dispute that some people are more fortunate than others, but they cannot control the circumstances which they were born into. Some individuals are raised in poverty, grow up without a father in the home, have lower cognitive abilities, and statistically speaking have a lower chance of becoming a doctor, lawyer or engineer. Yet, even while the chips may be stacked against a particular individual, the notion that systemic racism, gender inequality, bigotry, or Wall Street is to blame is simply not a productive policy subscription.

As the economist Thomas Sowell said, "Liberals seem to assume that if you don't believe in their particular political solutions, then you don't really care about the people that they claim to want to help."[lxxxviii] Conservatives would do well to steal Nike's "Just Do It slogan," and remind Millennials that when liberal politicians want them to claim victimhood, they can still work hard to finish high school, get a job, and wait until after they finish school before having babies. Placing faith on government handouts, and politicians who are more interested in votes is not the answer. As Sowell noted, "Elected officials, cannot readily admit that some policy or program that they advocated, perhaps with great fanfare, has turned out badly, without risking their whole careers."[lxxxix]

While an evil and hateful group known as the alt-right has distorted President Trump's rhetoric and turned it into a rallying cry for white nationalism, racism, bigotry, and xenophobia, they do not in any way resemble true conservative values and should be excoriated and demonized by any serious conservative. The alt-right is a group of disenfranchised individuals who are using the tactics of victimization. Although the media has long tried to paint vast swaths of conservatives as white supremacists, the conservative commentator Ben Shapiro articulated it is often the left that sows divisions and tears people apart:

> It is the left that tells Americans that political unity is more important than freedom of speech. It is the left that uses the clubs of race and class to attack those on the right; it is the left that labels religious people and traditional values people rubes and simpletons, and tells them that their perspective has no place in the public square; it is the left that creates environmental crises out of whole cloth, then rams remunerative measures down our collective throats. It is the left that tells us that it is unpatriotic to be patriotic. And most of all, it is the left that uses our most powerful institutions the institutions through which we connect with each other and build common bonds to tear us apart.[xc]

Only self-determination and personal responsibility can lift an individual up through the depths of despondency. If conservatives truly want to appeal to Millennials voters, then they must argue on moral terms and use language that resonates with younger voters. Conservatives must espouse religious freedom, while also expressing tolerance and inclusion of differing viewpoints. They must elucidate conservative values, liberty and free market principles, and the "Reaganism" that the government that governs least is the best form of democracy. As Shapiro noted:

> Capitalism is good because you own your own labor and you have the right to exchange that labor for someone else's labor and no one has the right to steal your labor from you. Socialism is evil because it says that a third party can tell you what your labor is worth. Religious freedom is good because freedom of association is good and no one has the right to tell you how to live your life so long as you're not forcibly imposing your views on anyone else. Governmental discrimination against religious institutions is evil because it is none of the government's business how you choose to worship, how you choose to operate your business, and how you choose to raise

your child. Freedom of speech is good because you have value as an individual human being with a unique point of view; you're not reducible to your skin color, your ethnicity, or your income. Political correctness and identity politics are evil because they utilize censorship to box you into a group identity that denies your individuality. Small government is good because it allows you to pursue your goals without someone else telling you what to do... Big government is evil because it insists that a cadre of bureaucrats knows more about how to run your life than you do.

CONTRIBUTION TO THE FIELD

This paper contributes to the field of Public Relations by researching and studying implicit and explicit instances of mainstream media bias and evaluating the adverse impact that this has had on the Conservative party. Public Relations is primarily concerned with reputation building and fostering a robust relationship with key stakeholders in a way that best informs and influences the public about the values, mission and philosophy of an organization or company. It is concluded that left wing mainstream media bias has hurt Conservative ideologies, leaders, and principles and has severely marginalized their reputation, particularly amongst Millennials.

This paper also contributes to the field of Public Relations by analyzing the communication channels where Millennials receive most of their news from, determining who or what is influencing their political habits or preferences, and the impact of mainstream media bias on their voting habits. This research was conducted to help Conservatives determine how they can best appeal to the hearts and minds of Millennial voters in future elections.

CRITICS OF LIBERAL MAINSTREAM MEDIA BIAS

Some researchers in academia contend that news outlets that are biased in favor of liberal viewpoints will alienate large segments of news consumers, result in smaller audiences, and reduce advertising revenues and profit. In other words, owners of news organizations such as NBC or CNN will not allow their staff to engage in advocacy journalism if that will hurt the bottom line.[xci] Daniel Sutter, a critic of liberal media bias, wrote that "If all current organizations present liberal news, a single right-of-center organization would have half of the political spectrum to themselves. The only conservative firm in a liberal-dominated market could likely draw larger audiences than possible as a member of the cartel." Indeed, the monopoly of liberal media outlets has in fact paved the way for a "single right-of-center organization," called Fox News, which has had more viewers of any news channel in the last sixteen years, and had six of the top ten most viewed cable news shows in 2018.[xcii] However, evidenced by the success of Fox News, and the media's overtly one-sided coverage of President Trump, news organization owners do seem willing to sacrifice revenue and/or alienate large segments of the population in order to support a political agenda.

Eric Alterman, a journalist and professor and one of the most notable scholars and critics of liberal media bias wrote a book entitled *What Liberal Media,* in which he characterized claims of a liberal media bias as nothing more than a "phony accusation" of seismic proportions. Alterman postulates that conservatives cry wolf about a supposed liberal media bias as a political strategy to rile up their base and "work the refs," in order to help their side win. He also wondered how a book by Ann Coulter, a conservative, or Bernard Goldberg, a critic of the mainstream media, could be a New York Times bestseller if a liberal media really existed.[xciii] Notably however, Alterman did not explain the correlation between books that consumers choose to buy, and the lack of objectivity by the mainstream media.

Alterman also claims that the conservative media is much larger than most people believe and receives far more funding than the liberal media:

> Given the success of Fox News, the Wall Street Journal editorial pages, the Washington Times, the New York Post, The American Spectator, The Weekly Standard, the New York Sun, National Review, Commentary, Limbaugh, Drudge, etc., no sensible person can dispute the existence of a "conservative media." The reader might be surprised to learn that neither do I quarrel with the notion of a "liberal media." It is tiny and profoundly underfunded compared with its conservative counterpart, but it does exist.[xciv]

No one with a reasonable level of integrity contends that conservative media outlets do not exist. The issue is that with the exception of Fox News, the Wall Street Journal, and the New York Post, most of the outlets that Alterman lists are hardly mainstream. The New York Sun now only exists in an online format and the Weekly Standard has since shutdown. It is unlikely that "the conservative media" that Alterman alluded to has anywhere near the reach or number of viewers as mainstream liberal outlets. The Wall Street Journal has two million subscribers, many of whom work in the financial industry and do not share the views that are espoused by the editorial.[xcv] The New York Post only has a print circulation of 422,000, but has a larger online presence.[xcvi] Meanwhile, the Washington Times has a circulation of just 85,000.[xcvii]

By contrast, the left-leaning New York Times has four million subscribers, the anti-President Trump Washington Post has over one million subscribers, the Los Angeles Times has a daily readership of 2.1 million, and USA Today has a circulation of over two million.[xcviii] [xcix] [c] [ci] Alterman also did not include that most of these conservative outlets, such as National Review or Drudge, make no qualms about their political agenda, and do not report under the guise of objectivity. As Brent Bozell, the founder of the RNC elucidated:

> Assuming Fox were as conservative as liberals charge and it's an assumption I am not willing to make, it would now be one against CBS, NBC, ABC, CNBC, MSNBC, CNN, CNN Headline News, and on and on and on. Some conservative dominance... What about Rush and the seemingly endless list of conservatives in the media today, men and women like Cal Thomas, Bob Novak, Michael Reagan, Laura Ingraham, and the like? All have two things in common: All openly, cheerfully acknowledge their biases; and all are commentators.
> Not a one is a member of the 'news media.'[cii]

CONCLUSION

The core values and ideologies of conservativism have suffered irreputable damage as a result of bias that is prevalent in mainstream media outlets, including the New York Times, Washington Post, CBS, NBC, ABC and CNN. The consistent and perpetual bias of the mainstream media has had an adverse effect on the Conservative party, especially with younger cohorts. Millennials, particularly ones with college degrees, are far more likely to identify as left wing or liberal and are more likely to vote for Democrats than to identify as Conservative and vote for Republican candidates. Fifty seven percent of Millennials hold consistently liberal values, while just twelve percent hold consistently conservative values.[ciii] This is especially problematic for the Conservative party in that numerous studies indicate Millennials will surpass baby boomers in 2019 as the largest class of voters.[civ]

Primary research for this paper shows that seventy percent of Millennials believe that the mainstream media, including the New York Times, Washington Post, CNN, ABC, CBS, and NBC has a liberal bias, however fifty eight percent of Millennials also believe that the mainstream media provides fair and accurate coverage of President Trump. In other words, Millennials agree that the mainstream media is biased, yet because their dislike for President Trump is so strong, they believe, inconsistently that news coverage of him is fair. Forty four percent of respondents mostly receive their political news and information from print and online newspapers. This indicates that traditional media still has a strong impact as a viable news source for Millennials. However, thirty percent of Millennials receive their political news and information from Twitter and Facebook and that number is likely to increase in the future.

Fifty percent of Millennials identified themselves as either liberal or Democratic, while just seventeen percent identified themselves as conservative or Republican. Seventy-two percent of Millennials said that they were likely to vote Democratic in the next election and seventy-six percent said they were either unlikely or extremely unlikely to vote for President Trump in the 2020 election. Thus, even Millennials who did not have a political affiliation with the Democratic or Republican party are still more likely to vote for a Democrat in an election.

Sixty- four percent of Millennials agreed with Bill Clinton's immigration stance. However, when that stance has been echoed by President Trump, Millennials rejected it. Seventy seven percent of participants agreed with an anonymous quote that Barack Obama made regarding his foreign policy strategy and fifty percent of Millennials agreed with a pro capitalist and free market statement from the economist Milton Friedman. Millennials' overwhelming support for these three statements, which focus on border and national security, as well as free markets proves part of the hypothesis of this paper, which is that when Millennials focus less on the speaker and more on the content proposed, their political views are more centrist on several important conservative issues. This suggests that Millennials could be persuaded to support certain conservative policies if they are worded in a way that resonates with them. However, sixty percent of Millennials disagreed with the assessment that their views are mostly shaped by the news media. This empirical evidence contradicts the other part of the hypothesis of the paper, which said that "the vast majority of Millennials do not identify as conservatives primarily due to false and defamatory charges that are pontificated through the national media." In other words, forty-seven percent of Millennials believe that friends and family are most responsible for their political views and not the mainstream media. While it is difficult to measure, it is likely that the thirty-four percent of Millennials who cited the New York Times as their primary news source will be heavily influenced by the content of it.

Only seven percent of journalists identify as Conservative or as Republicans.[cv] This disparity has had an adverse on conservative principles, figures, and ideologies. The RMC concluded that there are three major conflicts for so called objective journalists in the mainstream media. The first conflict: denial of liberal views or affiliation.[cvi] The second conflict: denying bias. The third conflict: lack of objective evaluation of a left leaning worldview with conservative viewpoints.

The RMC observed that there are a multitude of ways that the media can spin a news story to support left wing policies. It can decide to write about a specific political topic or policy from the perspective of liberal groups, or interview liberal policy experts, while disregarding conservative policy experts and studies done by right wing groups. The media can also influence public opinion by promoting negative stories about conservatives by placing them on the front pages of prominent newspapers, or by providing them with significant airtime on tv newscasts, while negative stories about liberals are provided much less prominence or ignored altogether.[cvii]

The latest IBD/TIPP poll shows that half of the country says that its trust in the media has decreased in the last two years and more than two-thirds believe the media is more concerned with pushing its own agenda instead of solely reporting the facts.[cviii] The mainstream media's reporting of the Jussie Smollett hate crime hoax, the Brett Kavanaugh sexual assault allegations and the vilification of the Covington Catholic students, has certainly helped to erode the public's faith in the media to report fairly and accurately.

Now that the Mueller Investigation has concluded, and the report "did not establish that members of the Trump Campaign conspired or coordinated with the Russian government in its election interference activities," Rachael Maddow of MSNBC and the rest of the mainstream media that has spent the past two years portraying President Trump as a Russian pawn, will likely have to come up with a new way to impugn his character, his policies and anyone who supports his agenda.[cix]

As the left-wing journalist Matt Taibbi said of the national media and its role in perpetuating the President Trump Russian collusion narrative: "Nobody wants to hear this, but news that Special Prosecutor Robert Mueller is headed home without issuing new charges is a death-blow for the reputation of the American news media."[cx] Taibbi further postulated that Russiagate was this generations version of the Weapons of Mass Destruction fallacy (WMDS). While the reputation of the media suffered immensely once it became clear that Saddam Hussein did not in fact possess weapons of mass destruction, Taibbi believes that Russiagate has served as a death blow to the public's faith in the media to see them as anything other than partisan journalists who are complicit in pushing any narrative, no matter how ludicrous, in order to destroy President Trump and his followers. "As with most press coverage, there was little pretense that the Mueller probe was supposed to be a neutral fact-finding mission, as opposed to religious allegory, with Mueller cast as the hero sent to slay the monster."[cxi]

Although liberal mainstream media bias continues to be a huge concern for the destruction of the conservative brand with Millennials, social media bias and censorship has become the lefts new crusade against conservatives and free speech. Google, Facebook and Twitter, donate a disproportionate amount to of money to Democratic candidates. According to the Center for Responsive Politics, during the 2018 Midterm Elections, ninety eight percent of political contributions from Twitter employees went to Democratic candidates. Meanwhile, ninety six percent of Google employees and ninety four percent of Facebook employees donated to Democratic candidates.[cxii] These figures should put to rest any debate as to where the political allegiances lie at these large and powerful tech companies.

Dr. Robert Epstein, a research psychologist at the American Institute for Behavioral Research and Technology, and a Hillary Clinton supporter has done extensive research on the Search Engine Manipulation Effect (SEME) and Search Suggestion Effect (SSE). Epstein who was interviewed for this paper expressed concerns about tech companies and what he called the "unfettered power to censor any political candidate, political party, company, organization, or point of view they wish to censor." His research on SEME found that when one candidate is favored over the other, the voting preferences for undecided voters can shift by up to twenty percent, and by as much as eighty percent in some demographics.[cxiii]

Epstein's studies have also concluded that SSE can turn a fifty-fifty split amongst undecided voters into a ninety-ten split, without the user having any knowledge that their search suggestions are being manipulated.[cxiv] The empirical evidence shows that undecided voters are ten to fifteen times more likely to click on a negative search suggestion item about a particular candidate, as opposed to a positive search suggestion item. This can significantly impact certain demographic groups, or groups of voters that tech companies might want to influence in an election.

According to Dr. Epstein, in the summer of 2016, there was overwhelming evidence, that Google was suppressing negative search results for Hillary Clinton, but not for other presidential candidates, including President Trump. Google defended its practices by saying that the users themselves were biased in favor of Hillary Clinton. However, if that were true then the biased search results would only show up in blue states. Yet, Epstein's studies concluded that there were biased search results in both blue and red states.[cxv]

While many people have become alarmed about the rise in biased reporting or fake news stories, these large tech companies could potentially have a greater impact on influencing public opinions than partisan journalists. Those interested in seeking the truth about what did or did not happen to Jussie Smollett and the Covington students can seek it out by exploring different media outlets, instead of taking CNN's word for it. Epstein does not believe that fake news is a very powerful way to shift public opinion or votes in an election, because it is a competitive process where one organization can compete with another to place their stories in a public environment. The much greater concern is the immense power that these tech companies have with how they manipulate their search suggestions and control the order in which stories are presented. Google is a tool that is designed around bias and makes decisions about what is worth seeing and what is worth seeing first. This can impact people's thinking, beliefs, attitudes, and decisions. As Epstein described it:

> The problem is that the platform itself eliminates the possibility of competition. If the platform itself only wants to allow fake news stories that favor one particular candidate, or one particular perspective, then there's nothing you can do. There is no way you can counter that. So now we're back to not really fake news stories being the issue, we're back to search results, and search suggestions, and answer boxes, we're back to seeing the search engine manipulation effect, the search suggestion effect. It's not the content that matters. It's not fake news that matters, because they're bound to be competing and different fake news stories out there. All that matters are the platforms and how they decide to display content. You can't counteract that with your own fake news stories if the platform itself is not going to let people see your content...you cannot control it if the platform takes a side... I'm still not concerned about fake news. I'm concerned about the platform and the unregulated power that the platforms have, to determine what people see and what they don't see, and the order in which they see content. That's where the power lies.

With the 2020 Presidential Election rapidly approaching, the mainstream media will likely play a significant role in determining whether President Trump will be re-elected, but Google, Facebook, and Twitter will likely play a larger role. Will Google continue to suppress negative search suggestions for Democratic candidates? Will Mark Zuckerberg send a go vote remainder to more liberal voters than conservative voters on election day? Will Twitter remove trending content from conservative thought leaders that it considers offensive, while holding liberal thought leaders to a different standard? These are important questions to consider, with serious consequences that every American in a free and democratic society should be concerned about.

PRIMARY RESEARCH GRAPHS:

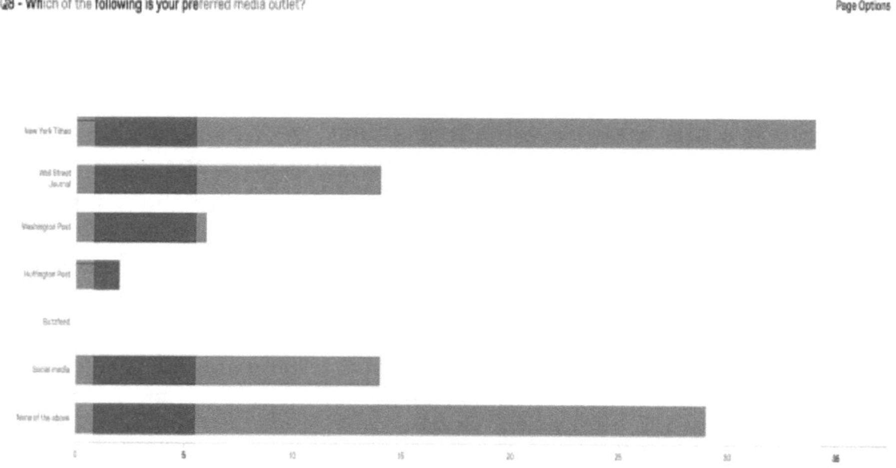

Table 1: Preferred media outlets for Millennials

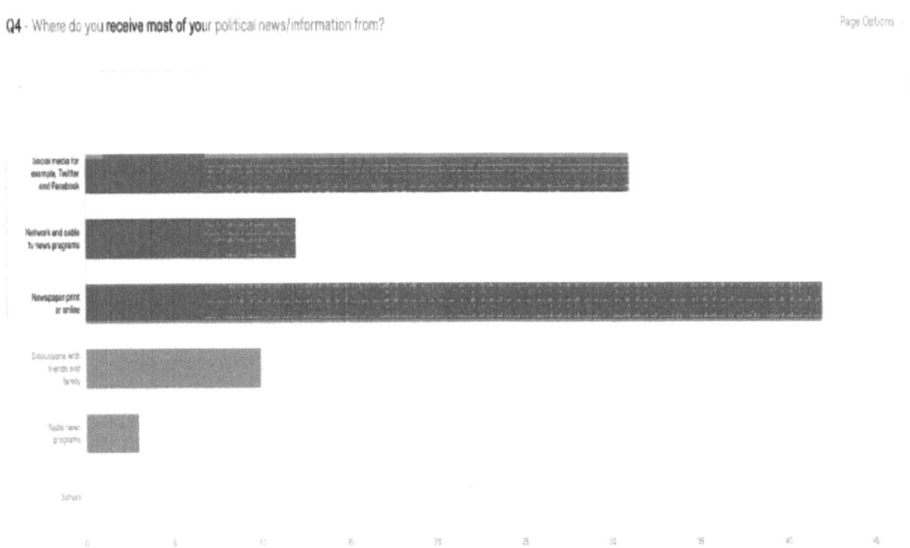

Table 2: Most popular political/news channels for Millennials

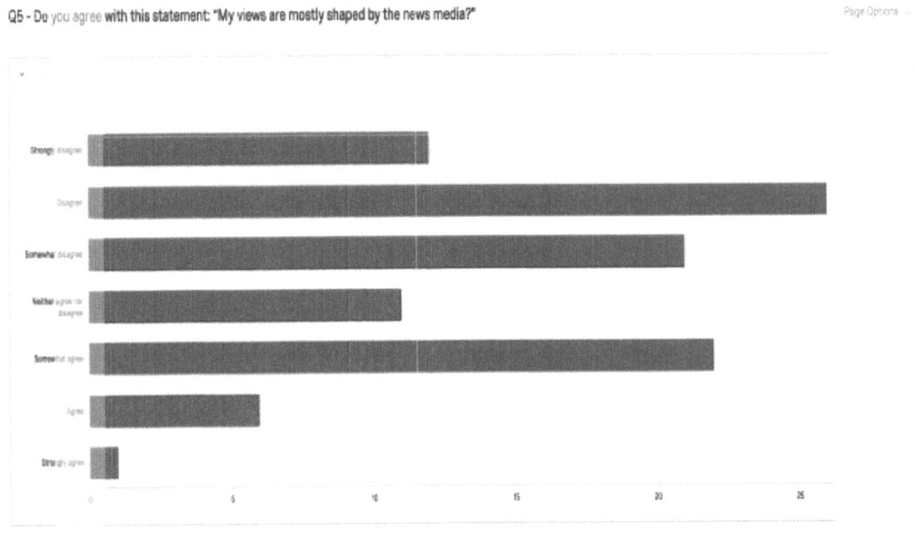

Table 3: The impact of the news media on Millennial viewpoints

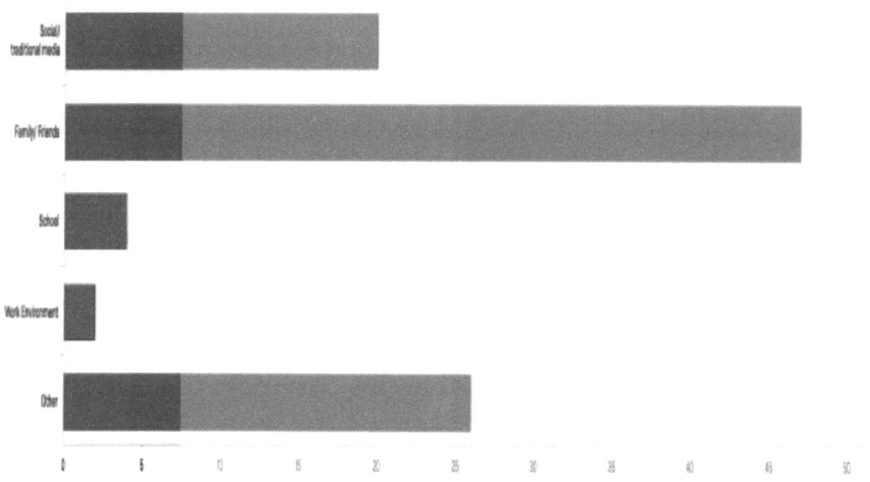

Table 4: Most likely to influence the political views of Millennials

Q7 - Would you agree or disagree that the mainstream media, including the New York Times, Washington Post, CNN, ABC, CBS, and NBC has a liberal bias? Page Options

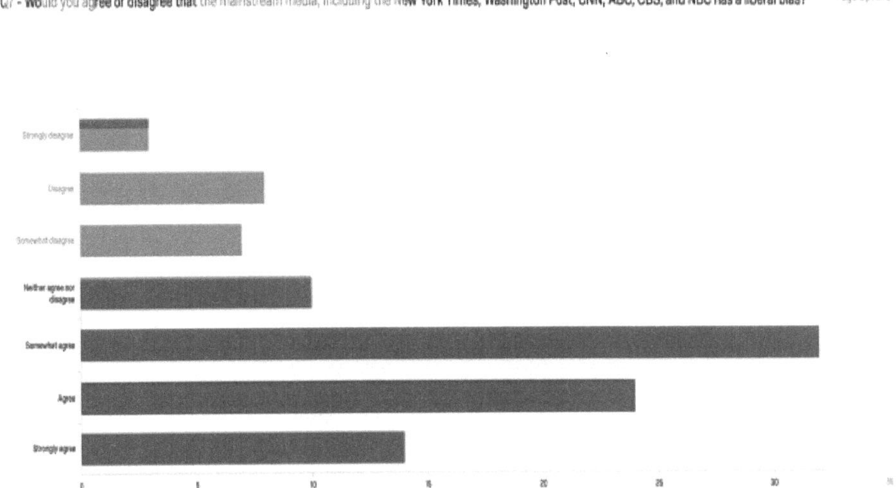

Table 5: Millennials perception of liberal media bias

Q9 - Do you believe that the mainstream media provides fair and accurate coverage of President Donald Trump? Page Options

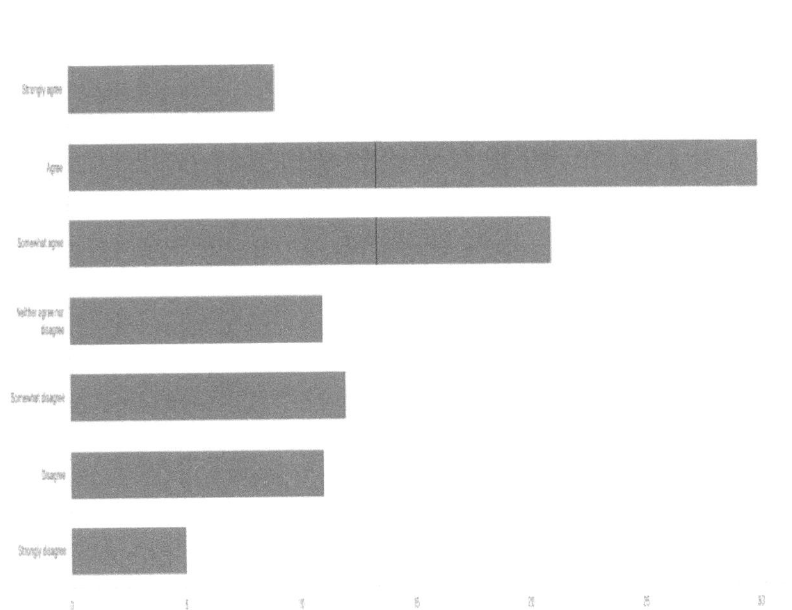

Table 6: Percentage of Millennials who believe that the mainstream media provides fair and accurate coverage of President Trump

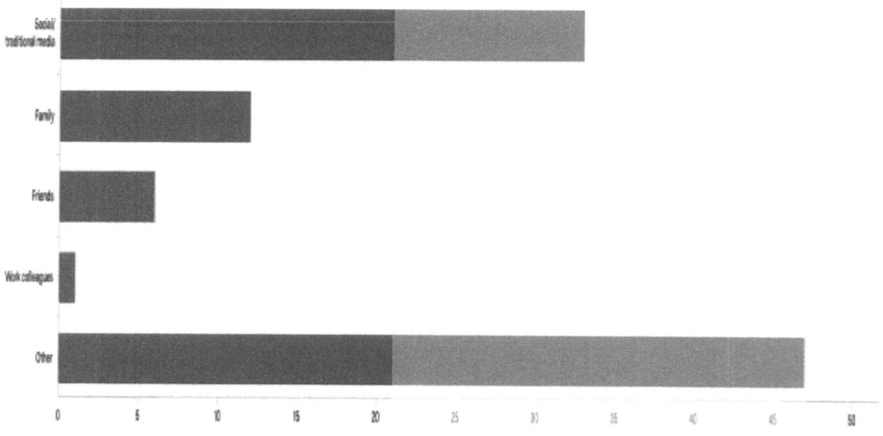

Table 7: Which factors will determine who Millennials vote for in 2020 election?

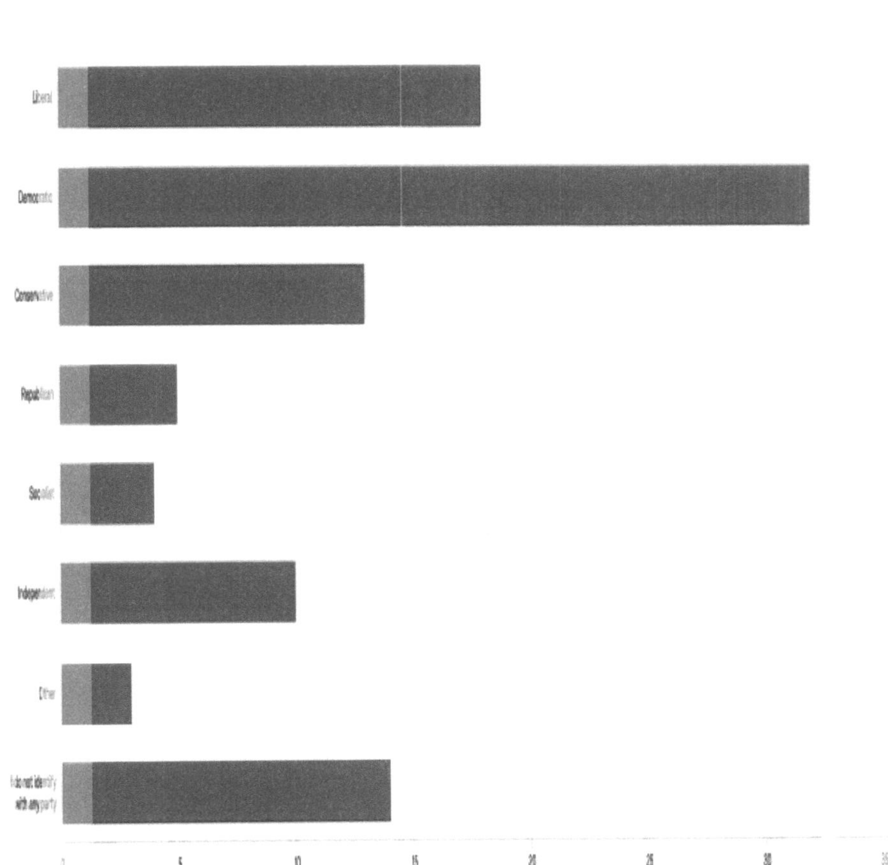

**Table 8: Which party most closely aligns with
Millennials political identity?**

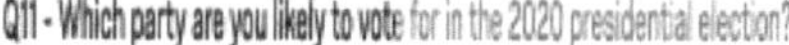

Table 9: Which political party are Millennials likely to vote for in the 2020 presidential election?

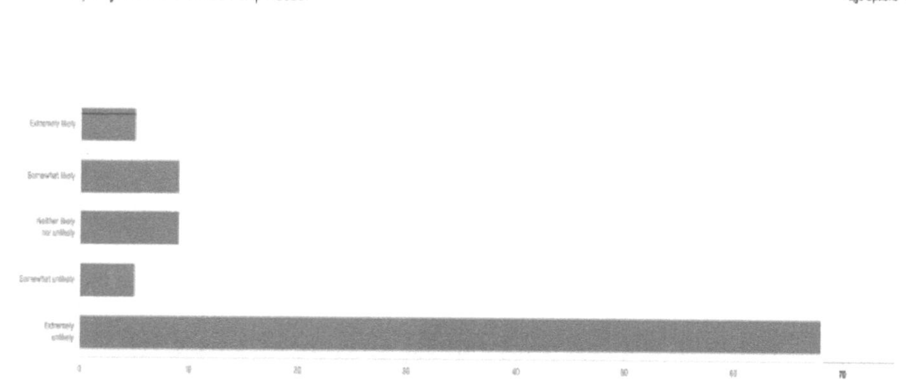

Table 10: Will Millennials vote for Donald Trump in 2020?

REFERENCES

[i] /pages/John-Merline/488385374573840. (2019, February 04). Media Bias: The Press Needs More Than A Super Bowl Ad To Fix Its Plunging Credibility. Retrieved from https://www.investors.com/politics/editorials/super-bowl-ad-media-bias/

[ii] Cillizza, C. (2014, May 06). Just 7 percent of journalists are Republicans. That's far fewer than even a decade ago. Retrieved from https://www.washingtonpost.com/news/the-fix/wp/2014/05/06/just-7-percent-of-journalists-are-republicans-thats-far-less-than-even-a-decade-ago/?noredirect=on&utm_term=.90f7ba341a56

[iii] The Generation Gap in American Politics. (2019, January 18). Retrieved from http://www.people-press.org/2018/03/01/the-generation-gap-in-american-politics/

[iv] Fry, R. (2018, April 03). Millennials approach Baby Boomers as America's largest generation in electorate. Retrieved from http://www.pewresearch.org/fact-tank/2018/04/03/Millennials-approach-baby-boomers-as-largest-generation-in-u-s-electorate/

[v] CNBC. (2015, October 28). Rubio: Democrats Have Ultimate Super PAC, The Mainstream Media | GOP Debate | CNBC. Retrieved from https://www.youtube.com/watch?v=QYdHHy9nnds

[vi] Cillizza, C. (2014, May 06). Just 7 percent of journalists are Republicans. That's far fewer than even a decade ago. Retrieved from https://www.washingtonpost.com/news/the-fix/wp/2014/05/06/just-7-percent-of-journalists-are-republicans-thats-far-less-than-even-a-decade-ago/?noredirect=on&utm_term=.90f7ba341a56

[vii] Media Research Center. (n.d.). Retrieved from https://www.mrc.org/

[viii] Goldberg, B. (2002). Bias: A CBS insider exposes how the media distort the

news. Washington DC: Regnery Publishing.

[ix] Goldberg, B. (2002). Bias: A CBS insider exposes how the media distort the news. Washington DC: Regnery Publishing.

[x] Goldberg, B. (2002). Bias: A CBS insider exposes how the media distort the news. Washington DC: Regnery Publishing.

[xi] The Generation Gap in American Politics. (2019, January 18). Retrieved from http://www.people-press.org/2018/03/01/the-generation-gap-in-american-politics/

[xii] Fry, R. (2018, April 03). Millennials approach Baby Boomers as America's largest generation in electorate. Retrieved from http://www.pewresearch.org/fact-tank/2018/04/03/Millennials-approach-baby-boomers-as-largest-generation-in-u-s-electorate/

[xiii] Media Research Center. (n.d.). Retrieved from https://www.mrc.org/

[xiv] Cillizza, C. (2014, May 06). Just 7 percent of journalists are Republicans. That's far fewer than even a decade ago. Retrieved from https://www.washingtonpost.com/news/the-fix/wp/2014/05/06/just-7-percent-of-journalists-are-republicans-thats-far-less-than-even-a-decade-ago/?noredirect=on&utm_term=.90f7ba341a56

[xv] Media Research Center. (n.d.). Retrieved from https://www.mrc.org/

[xvi] Media Research Center. (n.d.). Retrieved from https://www.mrc.org/

[xvii] Media Research Center. (n.d.). Retrieved from https://www.mrc.org/

[xviii] Goldberg, B. (2002, January 03). Networks Need a Reality Check. Retrieved from https://www.wsj.com/articles/SB1226696961168929319

[xix] New York Times Endorsements Through the Ages. (2016, September 23). Retrieved from https://www.nytimes.com/interactive/2016/09/23/opinion/presidential-endorsement-timeline.html

[xx] Concha, J. (2017, February 22). The Washington Post: 'Democracy dies in darkness'. Retrieved from https://thehill.com/homenews/media/320619-the-washington-post-democracy-dies-in-darkness

[xxi] Goldberg, B. (2002). Bias: A CBS insider exposes how the media distort the news. Washington DC: Regnery Publishing.

[xxii] Hanson, V. D., & Hanson, V. D. (2019, March 07). Donald Trump Promised to Drain the Swamp. Retrieved from https://www.nationalreview.com/2019/03/donald-trump-disruptor-drain-washington-swamp/

[xxiii] Cillizza, C. (2014, May 06). Just 7 percent of journalists are Republicans. That's far fewer than even a decade ago. Retrieved from https://www.washingtonpost.com/news/the-fix/wp/2014/05/06/just-7-percent-of-journalists-are-republicans-thats-far-less-than-even-a-decade-ago/?noredirect=on&utm_term=.90f7ba341a56

[xxiv] Reeve, E. (2013, October 29). Rick Stengel Is at Least the 24th Journalist to Work for the Obama Administration. Retrieved from https://www.theatlantic.com/politics/archive/2013/09/rick-stengel-least-24-journalist-go-work-obama-administration/310928/

[xxv] Smith, D. (2001, September 11). No Regrets for a Love Of Explosives; In a Memoir of Sorts, a War Protester Talks of Life With the Weathermen. Retrieved from https://www.nytimes.com/2001/09/11/books/no-regrets-for-love-explosives-memoir-sorts-war-protester-talks-life-with.html

[xxvi] Mullrainee. (2019, March 14). Why Al Sharpton's Race-Baiting Circus Should've Ended 25 Years Ago. Retrieved from https://mic.com/articles/58189/why-al-sharpton-s-race-baiting-circus-should-ve-ended-25-years-ago#.IQjAQedyc

[xxvii] (n.d.). Retrieved from https://abcnews.go.com/Blotter/DemocraticDebate/story?id=4443788&page=1

[xxviii] Kass, J. (2018, June 16). Obama's silky lie and FBI bias in the Clinton investigation. Retrieved from https://www.chicagotribune.com/news/columnists/kass/ct-met-james-comey-report-kass-0617-story.html

[xxix] Samuels, D. (2016, May 05). The Aspiring Novelist Who Became Obama's Foreign-Policy Guru. Retrieved from https://www.nytimes.com/2016/05/08/magazine/the-aspiring-novelist-who-became-obamas-foreign-policy-guru.html

[xxx] ISIS Fast Facts. (2019, January 21). Retrieved from https://www.cnn.com/2014/08/08/world/isis-fast-facts/index.html

[xxxi] President Obama. (2009, January 21). Retrieved from https://www.nytimes.com/2009/01/21/opinion/21wed1.html

[xxxii] Baker, P., & Michael. (2017, January 20). Donald Trump Is Sworn In as President, Capping His Swift Ascent. Retrieved from https://www.nytimes.com/2017/01/20/us/politics/trump-inauguration-day.html

[xxxiii] Williamson, E. (2017, August 26). President Trump and the Baby-Sitters Club. Retrieved from https://www.nytimes.com/2017/08/26/opinion/sunday/president-trump-and-the-baby-sitters-club.html

[xxxiv] Karni, A., & Altman, L. K. (2019, February 15). At 243 Pounds, Trump Tips the Scale Into Obesity. Retrieved from https://www.nytimes.com/2019/02/14/us/politics/trump-obese.html

[xxxv] Collins, G. (2019, January 10). Trump Hits the Wall. Retrieved from https://www.nytimes.com/2019/01/09/opinion/trump-border-speech.html

[xxxvi] Lord, D., & Cox Media Group National Content Desk. (2019, January 26). Trump border wall speech: Read the full transcript. Retrieved from https://www.ajc.com/news/national/trump-border-wall-speech-read-the-full-transcript/Zm6DfoKTbOb6mOvzxOBLwI/

[xxxvii] Lord, D., & Cox Media Group National Content Desk. (2019, January 26). Trump border wall speech: Read the full transcript. Retrieved from https://www.ajc.com/news/national/trump-border-wall-speech-read-the-full-transcript/Zm6DfoKTbOb6mOvzxOBLwI/

[xxxviii] Hinz, G. (2017, December 06). Invoking the specter of Nazi Germany, Obama warns against complacency. Retrieved from https://www.chicagobusiness.com/article/20171206/BLOGS02/171209933/barack-obama-invokes-nazi-germany-in-economic-club-remarks

[xxxix] Charles. (2018, January 15). Trump Is a Racist. Period. Retrieved from https://www.nytimes.com/2018/01/14/opinion/trump-racist-shithole.html

[xl] (n.d.). Retrieved from https://clintonwhitehouse4.archives.gov/textonly/WH/New/other/sotu.html

[xli] Lind, D. (2016, April 28). The disastrous, forgotten 1996 law that created today's immigration problem. Retrieved from https://www.vox.com/2016/4/28/11515132/iirira-clinton-immigration

[xlii] Mitchell, A., Matsa, K. E., Gottfried, J., Stocking, G., Grieco, E., Mitchell, A., . . . Grieco, E. (2017, October 02). Comparing news coverage of Trump's first 100 days to coverage of past administrations. Retrieved from https://www.journalism.org/2017/10/02/a-comparison-to-early-coverage-of-past-administrations/

[xliii] Victor Davis Hanson: The Case For Trump. (n.d.). Retrieved from https://www.hoover.org/research/victor-davis-hanson-case-trump

[xliv] Notable misstatements about Donald Trump from 2017. (n.d.). Retrieved from https://www.politifact.com/truth-o-meter/article/2017/dec/12/notable-misstatements-about-donald-trump-2017/

[xlv] Michael. (2017, December 08). CNN Corrects a Trump Story, Fueling Claims of 'Fake News'. Retrieved from https://www.nytimes.com/2017/12/08/business/media/cnn-correction-donald-trump-jr.html

[xlvi] News, A. (2019, February 15). Jussie Smollett FULL Interview on alleged attack | ABC News Exclusive. Retrieved from https://www.youtube.com/watch?v=pXLx5OY21Bk

[xlvii] Booker, C. (2019, January 29). The vicious attack on actor Jussie Smollett was an attempted modern-day lynching. I'm glad he's safe.To those in Congress who don't fethe urgency to pass our Anti-Lynching bill designating lynching as a federal hate crime– I urge you to pay attention. https://t.co/EwXFxl5f2m. Retrieved from https://twitter.com/corybooker/status/1090341255786184704?lang=

[xlviii] Nickolai, N., & Nickolai, N. (2019, February 23). Kamala Harris 'Frustrated and Disappointed' by Jussie Smollett Allegedly Staging Attack. Retrieved from https://variety.com/2019/politics/news/kamala-harris-jussie-smollett-staged-attack-1203146430/

[xlix] News, F. (2019, February 18). Tucker sounds off on new Jussie Smollett developments. Retrieved from https://www.youtube.com/watch?v=ue5i_9b7Bm4

[l] Brown, E. (2018, September 16). California professor, writer of confidential Brett Kavanaugh letter, speaks out about her allegation of sexual assault. Retrieved from https://www.washingtonpost.com/investigations/california-professor-writer-of-confidential-brett-kavanaugh-letter-speaks-out-about-her-allegation-of-sexual-assault/2018/09/16/46982194-b846-11e8-94eb-3bd52dfe917b_story.html?

noredirect=on&utm_term=.ab13fa9ad7ce

[li] Gersen, J. S., & Gersen, J. S. (2018, September 25). Deborah Ramirez's Allegation Against Brett Kavanaugh Raises Classic Questions of Campus Assault Cases. Retrieved from https://www.newyorker.com/news/our-columnists/deborah-ramirezs-allegation-against-brett-kavanaugh-raises-classic-questions-of-campus-assault-cases

[lii] Fandos, N., & Edmondson, C. (2018, August 11). 'So, So Jaded': The Campaign to Stop Brett Kavanaugh Struggles for Liftoff. Retrieved from https://www.nytimes.com/2018/08/11/us/politics/brett-kavanaugh-supreme-court-fight.html

[liii] The New York Times. (2018, September 26). Brett Kavanaugh's Opening Statement: Full Transcript. Retrieved from https://www.nytimes.com/2018/09/26/us/politics/read-brett-kavanaughs-complete-opening-statement.html

[liv] Baker, P. (2018, September 27). She Said. Then He Said. Now What Will Senators Say? Retrieved from https://www.nytimes.com/2018/09/27/us/politics/dr-blasey-ford-testimony-kavanaugh.html

[lv] Government, T. C. (2018, September 27). Kavanaugh hearing: Transcript. Retrieved from https://www.washingtonpost.com/news/national/wp/2018/09/27/kavanaugh-hearing-transcript/?utm_term=.af06a5d59a81

[lvi] Goldberg, J., & Goldberg, J. (2018, October 04). Kavanaugh coverage reveals huge problem within the Fourth Estate. Retrieved from https://nypost.com/2018/10/03/kavanaugh-coverage-reveals-huge-problem-within-the-fourth-estate/
[lvii]

[lviii] CNN. (2018, October 01). Don Lemon: This is not McCarthyism, but search for truth. Retrieved from https://www.youtube.com/watch?v=cTo8j9WD04k
[lix] CNN. (2018, October 04). Chris Cuomo: Kavanaugh is who he was in that hearing. Retrieved from https://www.youtube.com/watch?v=uWWdup0EfLg

[lx] Goldberg, J., & Goldberg, J. (2018, October 03). You Idiot Reporters Are Making It Worse. Retrieved from https://www.nationalreview.com/2018/10/kavanaugh-hearings-partisan-reporters-making-it-worse/
[lxi] NewsHour, P. (2018, October 05). Feinstein says Kavanaugh has not 'earned' his seat on Supreme Court. Retrieved from https://www.youtube.com/watch?v=Er1Dhsw00Zk

[lxii] Mitchell, R. (2018, September 30). Analysis of Dr. Christine Blasey Ford's Allegations. Retrieved February 25, 2019, from https://assets.documentcloud.org/documents/4952137/Rachel-Mitchell-s-analysis.pdf

[lxiii] Board, T. E. (2018, September 28). Why Brett Kavanaugh Wasn't Believable. Retrieved from https://www.nytimes.com/2018/09/27/opinion/why-brett-kavanaugh-wasnt-believable.html

[lxiv] Mitchell, R. (2018, September 30). Analysis of Dr. Christine Blasey Ford's Allegations. Retrieved February 25, 2019, from https://assets.documentcloud.org/documents/4952137/Rachel-Mitchell-s-analysis.pdf

[lxv] Board, T. E. (2018, September 28). Why Brett Kavanaugh Wasn't Believable. Retrieved from https://www.nytimes.com/2018/09/27/opinion/why-brett-kavanaugh-wasnt-believable.html

[lxvi] Kavanaugh, B. M. (2018, October 04). Opinion | I Am an Independent, Impartial Judge. Retrieved from https://www.wsj.com/articles/i-am-an-independent-impartial-judge-1538695822

[lxvii] CNN. (2018, October 05). Susan Collins will vote to confirm Kavanaugh. Retrieved from https://www.youtube.com/watch?v=636n0XUx95o

[lxviii] News, F. (2019, January 21). Tucker: MAGA hat-wearing students smeared by media. Retrieved from https://www.youtube.com/watch?v=l3Zp4ldFC4w

[lxix] Smith, K., & Smith, K. (2019, January 21). Nathan Phillips Lied. The Media Bought It. Retrieved from https://www.nationalreview.com/2019/01/nathan-phillips-lied-the-media-bought-it/

[lxx] Marcos, C. (2019, January 28). Omar deletes tweet on Covington students, Trump. Retrieved from https://thehill.com/homenews/house/426635-omar-deletes-tweet-on-covington-students-trump

[lxxi] Aslan, R. (2019, January 20). Honest question. Have you ever seen a more punchable face than this kid's? pic.twitter.com/jolQ7BZQPD. Retrieved from https://twitter.com/rezaaslan/status/1086806539552284672?lang=en

[lxxii] Mikelionis, L. (n.d.). Journalist fired after wishing death on Covington Catholic HS students, parents: Report. Retrieved from https://www.foxnews.com/us/journalist-fired-from-job-after-wishing-death-for-covington-catholic-hs-students-parents

[lxxiii] Eligon, J. (2019, January 23). Hebrew Israelites See Divine Intervention in Lincoln Memorial Confrontation. Retrieved from https://www.nytimes.com/2019/01/23/us/black-hebrew-israelites-covington-catholic.html

[lxxiv] Pc, L. (2019, February 01). Nick Sandmann: The Truth in 15 Minutes. Retrieved from https://www.youtube.com/watch?v=lSkpPaiUF8s

[lxxv] TODAY. (2019, January 24). Native American Elder Nathan Phillips On Confrontation: 'I Forgive Him' | TODAY. Retrieved from https://www.youtube.com/watch?v=h-9-qmN0Hmw

[lxxvi] Statement of Nick Sandmann, Covington Catholic High School junior, regarding incident at the Lincoln Memorial. (2019, January 23). Retrieved from https://www.cnn.com/2019/01/20/us/covington-kentucky-student-statement/index.html

[lxxvii] Phung, A. (2019, February 20). Nick Sandmann files lawsuit against the Washington Post. Retrieved from https://www.cnn.com/2019/02/19/media/nick-sandmann-washington-post-lawsuit/index.html

[lxxviii] Darrah, N. (n.d.). Sandmann, family sue CNN for $275M in Covington Catholic controversy. Retrieved from https://www.foxnews.com/us/sandmann-family-sue-cnn-for-275m-in-covington-catholic-controversy

[lxxix] TODAY. (2019, January 23). Nick Sandmann Speaks Out On Viral Encounter With Nathan Phillips | TODAY. Retrieved from https://www.youtube.com/watch?v=c8ZhDGaQMS4&t=391s

[lxxx] TODAY. (2019, January 23). Nick Sandmann Speaks Out On Viral Encounter With Nathan Phillips | TODAY. Retrieved from https://www.youtube.com/watch?v=c8ZhDGaQMS4&t=391s

[lxxxi] Smith, K., & Smith, K. (2019, January 21). Nathan Phillips Lied. The Media Bought It. Retrieved from https://www.nationalreview.com/2019/01/nathan-phillips-lied-the-media-bought-it/

[lxxxii] TODAY. (2019, January 24). Native American Elder Nathan Phillips On Confrontation: 'I Forgive Him' | TODAY. Retrieved from https://www.youtube.com/watch?v=h-9-qmN0Hmw

[lxxxiii] Smith, K., & Smith, K. (2019, January 21). Nathan Phillips Lied. The Media Bought It. Retrieved from https://www.nationalreview.com/2019/01/nathan-phillips-lied-the-media-bought-it/

[lxxxiv] News, F. (2019, January 22). Levin slams liberal media, invites Ocasio-Cortez onto show. Retrieved from https://www.youtube.com/watch?v=iusrb0FyLPI

[lxxxv] Updated - Establish a ban on Muslims entering the U.S. (n.d.). Retrieved from https://www.politifact.com/truth-o-meter/promises/trumpometer/promise/1401/establish-ban-muslims-entering-us/

[lxxxvi] The Declaration of Independence: Full text. (n.d.). Retrieved from http://www.ushistory.org/declaration/document/

[lxxxvii] Edwards, L. (n.d.). What Is Conservatism? Retrieved from https://www.heritage.org/conservatism/commentary/what-conservatism

[lxxxviii] Thomas Sowell Quotes. (n.d.). Retrieved from https://www.brainyquote.com/authors/thomas_sowell

[lxxxix] Sowell, T. (2011). Economic facts and fallacies. New York: Basic Books.

[xc] Shapiro, B. (2014). Bullies: How the lefts culture of fear and intimidation silences America. New York: Threshold Editions.

[xci] Sutter, Daniel. "Can the Media be so Liberal? the Economics of Media Bias." Cato Journal, vol. 20, no. 3, 2001, pp. 431-451. ProQuest, http://proxy.library.nyu.edu/login?url=https://search.proquest.com/docview/195575491?accountid=12768

[xcii] Sutter, Daniel. "Can the Media be so Liberal? the Economics of Media Bias." Cato Journal, vol. 20, no. 3, 2001, pp. 431-451. ProQuest, http://proxy.library.nyu.edu/login?url=https://search.proquest.com/docview/195575491?accountid=12768.

[xciii] Sutter, Daniel. "Can the Media be so Liberal? the Economics of Media Bias." Cato Journal, vol. 20, no. 3, 2001, pp. 431-451. ProQuest, http://proxy.library.nyu.edu/login?url=https://search.proquest.com/docview/195575491?accountid=12768.

[xciv] Sutter, Daniel. "Can the Media be so Liberal? the Economics of Media Bias." Cato Journal, vol. 20, no. 3, 2001, pp. 431-451. ProQuest, http://proxy.library.nyu.edu/login?url=https://search.proquest.com/docview/195575491?accountid=12768.

[xcv] Wall Street Journal: Circulation 2018 | Statistic. (n.d.). Retrieved from https://www.statista.com/statistics/193788/average-paid-circulation-of-the-wall-street-journal/

[xcvi] https://muckrack.com/blog/2018/04/25/the-top-10-newspaper-publications-in-new-york

[xcvii] Washington Times. (n.d.). Retrieved from https://www.conserva-pedia.com/Washington_Times

[xcviii] Peiser, J. (2018, November 01). New York Times Tops 4 Million Mark in Total Subscribers. Retrieved from https://www.nytimes.com/2018/11/01/business/media/new-york-times-earnings-subscribers.html

[xcix] Year, ". T. (n.d.). Washington Post digital subscriptions soar past 1 million mark. Retrieved from https://money.cnn.com/2017/09/26/media/washington-post-digital-subscriptions/index.html

[c] About the Los Angeles Times and how to contact us. (2019, January 09). Retrieved from https://www.latimes.com/about/la-contact-us-htmlstory.html

[ci] USA Today. (2019, April 03). Retrieved from https://en.wikipedia.org/wiki/USA_Today

[cii] Foxtrot501. (2010, June 16). Are The Media Liberal? Retrieved from https://www.nationalreview.com/2003/02/are-media-liberal-foxtrot501/

[ciii] The Generation Gap in American Politics. (2019, January 18). Retrieved from http://www.people-press.org/2018/03/01/the-generation-gap-in-american-politics/

[civ] Fry, R. (2018, April 03). Millennials approach Baby Boomers as America's largest generation in electorate. Retrieved from http://www.pewresearch.org/fact-tank/2018/04/03/Millennials-approach-baby-boomers-as-largest-generation-in-u-s-electorate/

[cv] Cillizza, C. (2014, May 06). Just 7 percent of journalists are Republicans. That's far fewer than even a decade ago. Retrieved from https://www.washingtonpost.com/news/the-fix/wp/2014/05/06/just-7-percent-of-journalists-are-republicans-thats-far-less-than-even-a-decade-ago/?noredirect=on&utm_term=.90f7ba341a56

[cvi] Media Research Center. (n.d.). Retrieved from https://www.mrc.org/

[cvii] Media Research Center. (n.d.). Retrieved from https://www.mrc.org/

[cviii] /pages/John-Merline/488385374573840. (2019, February 04). Media Bias: The Press Needs More Than A Super Bowl Ad To Fix Its Plunging Credibility. Retrieved from https://www.investors.com/politics/editorials/super-bowl-ad-media-bias/

[cix] The New York Times. (2019, March 24). Read Attorney General William Barr's Summary of the Mueller Report. Retrieved from https://www.nytimes.com/interactive/2019/03/24/us/politics/barr-letter-mueller-report.html

[cx] It's official: Russiagate is this generation's WMD. (n.d.). Retrieved from https://taibbi.substack.com/p/russiagate-is-wmd-times-a-million

[cxi] It's official: Russiagate is this generation's WMD. (n.d.). Retrieved from https://taibbi.substack.com/p/russiagate-is-wmd-times-a-million

[cxii] Molla, R. (2018, October 31). Tech employees are much more liberal than their employers - at least as far as the candidates they support. Retrieved from https://www.recode.net/2018/10/31/18039528/tech-employees-politics-liberal-employers-candidates

[cxiii] 10 Ways Big Tech Can Shift Millions of Votes in the November Elections-Without Anyone Knowing. (2018, September 28). Retrieved from https://www.theepochtimes.com/10-ways-big-tech-can-shift-millions-of-votes-in-the-november-elections-without-anyone-knowing_2671195.html

[cxiv] 10 Ways Big Tech Can Shift Millions of Votes in the November Elections-Without Anyone Knowing. (2018, September 28). Retrieved from https://www.theepochtimes.com/10-ways-big-tech-can-shift-millions-of-votes-in-the-november-elections-without-anyone-knowing_2671195.html

[cxv] 10 Ways Big Tech Can Shift Millions of Votes in the November Elections-Without Anyone Knowing. (2018, September 28). Retrieved from https://www.theepochtimes.com/10-ways-big-tech-can-shift-millions-of-votes-in-the-november-elections-without-anyone-knowing_2671195.html